FROM GARDEN TO GRILL

ELIZABETH ORSINI

Over 250 Vegetable-based Recipes for every Grill Master

CIDER MILL PRESS

BOOK PUBLISHERS

KENNEBUNKPORT, MAINE

Cider Mill Press Book Publishers
"Where good books are ready for press"
PO Box 454
12 Spring St.
Kennebunkport, Maine 04046

Visit us on the Web!
www.cidermillpress.com

Special thanks to Whalen Book Works.
www.whalenbookworks.com

NEW YORK CITY, NEW YORK

Cover Design by Mallory Grigg
Interior design by Alicia Freile, Tango Media
Cover Images:
Top image used under license, Getty Images/Chris Stein/Creative # 82681030
Bottom image used under license, Getty Images/photo by tedfoo/Creative # 102941055
All images used under license from Shutterstock.com.

Typography: Blackout Midnight, Helvetica Rounded, Knockout, Minion, Neutraface, and Sentinal

Printed in China

2 3 4 5 6 7 8 9 0

AUG - 9 2019

For Kristin and Baroni

Contents

Introduction

The vibrant bounty of your vegetable garden deserves to be celebrated, and what better way than by introducing it to the grill—a cooking utensil so thoroughly commandeered by carnivores that we often forget its other wonderful applications. With this cookbook, I set out with one simple idea: Bring your harvest to life.

Not only does vegetarian grilling offer a more enticing way of getting the nutrients you need—there's also something beautiful about seeing the char lines appear on your vegetables; in delighting in their smokiness after you take them off the grill. And these recipes give you special ownership of your produce whether you've grown it yourself or not; creative and simple, they elevate even the most common store-bought greens.

Still, not everybody feels the same passion for vegetables, and I've written this book with every dietary preference in mind. With variations for carnivores, vegans and paleo and gluten-free eaters, these recipes are perfect for customization on any level. It's incredibly easy to swap out vegetables that you dislike for the ones that you love, as most vegetables cook very similarly. And for those that do need some meat in their meals, the techniques discussed in this book will help you grill smarter, keeping your proteins lean and your meals balanced.

Some recipes will require the use of additional materials, but that doesn't mean you need to break the bank on kitchen supplies. For instance, a grill basket is necessary for some of the recipes—you can substitute with a disposable foil pan by simply poking holes in the bottom of the pan to allow for drainage. Additionally, when grilling with skewers, I recommend using bamboo or metal, but you may not have those. As long as you're being safe, use whatever materials are available to you. No matter which utensils you use, your vegetables will still be the stars of the show.

Everyone's grill is different, but most vegetables are finished cooking once they can be easily pierced with a knife. Of course, the best way to check is a simple taste test— you get to steal an extra bite while ensuring that your vegetables are always grilled to the consistency of your choosing. It's also important to note the difference between grilling and barbecue. Barbecuing is a much slower method of cooking because the food is cooked indirectly, via convection. Grilling is much quicker because food is heated through conduction, meaning direct contact with its heat source. If you have doubts about your own grilling time, I encourage you to check for the temperature you prefer.

Not every recipe needs to reinvent the wheel, but they should all make you feel good. And they should be accessible to everybody, so the entire table gets to enjoy the magnificent yield from a lovingly tended vegetable garden. There are hundreds of recipes inside this book— find the ones that work for you and the hungry mouths at your table, and bring your garden to the dinner table. Happy grilling!

— Elizabeth

Substitutions

This section will break down the somewhat daunting process of making your very own substitutes! Alternatives for vegan, paleo and gluten-free diets are relatively easy to find in most supermarkets, but it's often just as simple to make many of them at home. These are very basic recipes that make for delicious options you can prepare hours or even days in advance. And like everything else in this book, these substitutes can be adjusted to fit your needs.

If you're eager to skip ahead to the complete recipes, feel free; I'll be sending you back here often as I offer variations to each recipe. It may seem burdensome to add extra work to a recipe, but remember: Give a man a gluten-free tortilla and feed him for a day. But teach him to make a gluten-free tortilla and feed him for life.

Cauliflower Gluten-Free Pizza Dough

ACTIVE TIME: 5 MINUTES • TOTAL TIME: 20 MINUTES • SERVES 4

This pizza dough is perfect for anyone following a gluten-free diet. Just make sure the cauliflower is completely dry before processing it.

1 standard bag of frozen cauliflower

¼ cup Parmesan cheese, grated

2 cups mozzarella, shredded

3 teaspoons oregano

1 teaspoon basil

½ teaspoon salt

1 clove garlic, minced

2 eggs, lightly beaten

1. Steam the cauliflower according to the directions on the package. Cook the cauliflower ahead of time and let it dry overnight on a sheet pan in the refrigerator, or let it cool and pat dry. This will help get all of the water out and keep the crust as crisp as possible.

2. Pulse the completely dry cauliflower in a food processor and add it to a large bowl.

3. Add the Parmesan, mozzarella, oregano, basil, salt, garlic and eggs. Mix well and transfer mixture to a baking sheet.

4. Spread it into a large circle and bake for 20 minutes. After adding your pizza toppings, cook for another 10 minutes on the grill over medium heat!

Paleo Pizza Dough

This Paleo Pizza Dough is also gluten-free, so you can alternate it with the cauliflower dough if it's more to your liking.

1. Preheat your grill or oven to high heat (450 degrees F). In a medium-sized bowl, combine the tapioca flour and $1/3$ cup of coconut flour. Mix well before adding the olive oil, water and whisked egg. Continue to mix until everything has blended evenly. While mixing, slowly add the 3 extra tablespoons of coconut flour until the dough thickens and becomes slightly sticky.

2. Sprinkle a little tapioca powder on a flat surface, place the mixture on top, and knead the dough until it becomes manageable and less sticky. Flour a rolling pin with tapioca flour and roll out the dough on a piece of parchment paper. This should give you about a 12-inch circular piece of dough.

3. Bake the dough for 12–15 minutes, or until it reaches desired crispness. This can also be cooked on the grill with the lid closed, but keep an eye on it to make sure it does not overcook.

4. Add toppings and grill for a few more minutes.

1 cup tapioca flour

$1/3$ cup coconut flour

3 tablespoons coconut flour

1 teaspoon salt

$1/2$ cup olive oil

$1/2$ cup warm water

1 large egg, whisked

Cauliflower Rice

A simple rice substitute that doesn't sacrifice flavor.

1 large head of cauliflower
3 teaspoon olive oil
Pinch of salt and pepper

1. In a food processor, pulse the cauliflower until it reduces to the size of grains.

2. In a skillet over medium heat, heat olive oil and cook your cauliflower rice for 3–5 minutes, covered. Sprinkle with salt and pepper to taste.

Vegan Parmesan Cheese

Vegan cheese may sound counterintuitive, but this recipe brings tons of flavor to a dish without masking its other components.

1 cup raw almonds, blanched
½ cup raw cashews
¼ cup nutritional yeast
½ teaspoon salt
¼ teaspoon garlic powder

In a food processor, pulse all of the ingredients until the blend becomes granular, resembling grated Parmesan. Store this for up to two months in the refrigerator.

Moxarella

This wonderfully textured vegan option can be sliced or grated, making it as dynamic as the real thing. Perhaps more so, considering the different diets it satisfies.

¼ cup raw cashews, soaked for several hours and drained

1 cup hot water

2 tablespoons tapioca flour

1 teaspoon tapioca flour

1 tablespoon olive oil

1 clove garlic, minced

¾ teaspoon salt

1 teaspoon lemon juice

1. In a high-powered blender, blend all the ingredients together until the mixture is completely smooth. This should take about 1 minute.

2. Pour mixture into a small saucepan and cook over medium-high heat for about 3 minutes. Be sure to stir constantly.

3. Once the mixture begins to look as though it's curdling, reduce the heat to medium and keep stirring. After 2–3 more minutes the mixture should get very thick, at which point you can remove from heat and let it cool.

Macadamia Ricotta Cheese

Vegans and paleo-eaters will want to memorize this five-minute recipe. In a pinch, it can take any dish to another level.

2 cups raw macadamia nuts

1 teaspoon kosher salt

1 tablespoon lemon juice

½ cup water

Combine all the ingredients in a food processor. Puree on high until the mixture becomes smooth. If necessary, add a bit more water.

Paleo and Gluten-Free Tortillas

ACTIVE TIME: 10 MINUTES • TOTAL TIME: 20 MINUTES • SERVES 6

Taking only 20 minutes to make, these tortillas save you a trip to the supermarket and work with most diets.

1. In a medium bowl, mix the eggs, coconut milk, coconut oil and water. Stir well before adding the rest of the ingredients. After mixing thoroughly, let the mixture sit for about 5 minutes.

2. Cook over medium heat in a medium-sized, non-stick pan. Pour 1/3 cup of the batter into the pan and swirl it immediately, filling the entire pan. Cook the batter for 1–2 minutes on each side, or until the tortilla has slightly browned. Remove from heat and repeat for the next tortilla.

2 eggs

1 cup coconut milk

1 tablespoon coconut oil

1 teaspoon water

½ cup tapioca flour

¼ cup almond flour

3 tablespoons coconut flour

Pinch of salt

Paleo Pizza Sauce

Though I reference this flavorful red sauce primarily during grilled pizza recipes, you'll find it makes a lovely addition to any Italian dish.

Mix all of the ingredients together in a medium bowl and let the sauce sit at room temperature until you're ready for it.

8 ounces tomato paste

½ cup tomato sauce

1 teaspoon salt

1 teaspoon dried oregano

1 teaspoon dried basil

1 clove garlic, minced

Paleo Basil Pesto

Because pesto does not keep for very long, you'll be well served by making your own rather than spending on the store-bought version.

Combine the non-liquid ingredients in a food processor and pulse until everything is evenly chopped. Slowly add the olive oil until the mixture becomes smooth. Serve and enjoy!

2 cups basil leaves

½ cup olive oil

⅓ cup pine nuts

3 cloves garlic, minced

Pinch of salt and pepper

Paleo Mayonnaise

ACTIVE TIME: 15 MINUTES • TOTAL TIME: 15 MINUTES • SERVES 1 CUP

To ensure this tasty mayonnaise alternative processes correctly, drizzle the oil in slowly until emulsified.

2 egg yolks

1 teaspoon mustard

3 teaspoons lemon juice

½ cup olive oil

½ cup coconut oil

Salt and pepper, to taste

1. Mix yolks, mustard and lemon juice in a food processor. Add the oil very slowly to keep it from separating during the mixing process.

2. Once the mixture starts to thicken, you can add the oil more quickly. Season with salt and pepper and enjoy.

Peachy Paleo Salsa

ACTIVE TIME: 20 MINUTES • TOTAL TIME: 20 MINUTES • SERVES 4

Peach salsa is already so refreshing—give yours that extra healthy kick by ensuring it is paleo-friendly.

4 peaches, diced

6 ounces blueberries

1 red onion, minced

1 clove garlic, minced

1 jalapeno pepper, minced

1 tablespoon fresh basil, minced

1 tablespoon fresh chives, minced

1 teaspoon cilantro, minced

3 tablespoons lime juice

¼ cup peach juice

In a medium bowl, combine all ingredients and serve.

Paleo Ketchup

Since off-the-shelf ketchup is filled with sugar, homemade Paleo Ketchup can be served as the only sauce you need. It's also super quick and easy to make!

6 ounces tomato paste

2 tablespoons lemon juice

¼ teaspoon dry mustard

⅓ cup water

¼ teaspoon salt

¼ teaspoon ground allspice

⅛ teaspoon cayenne pepper

¼ teaspoon ground cloves

Combine all ingredients in a small bowl and mix until the sauce is smooth. Refrigerate overnight.

Paleo Pork Chops

The trick to cooking pork chops isn't in the seasoning: Everything hinges on how long you cook the meat. Pork chops tend to dry out very suddenly—if you have a meat thermometer on hand, check the internal temperature regularly until it reads 145 degrees F, then remove from heat immediately.

2 cloves garlic, minced

1 cup fresh basil leaves, minced

2 tablespoons lemon juice

2 tablespoons olive oil

1 pinch salt and pepper

4 pork loin chops, bone-in

1. In a small bowl, combine the garlic, basil, lemon juice, olive oil, salt and pepper. Spread over the pork chops and marinate for 30–45 minutes.

2. Grill over medium heat for about 4 minutes on each side, or until the pork chops are tender.

Marinades & sauces

Beautifully grown greens deserve a sauce to match, and the contents of this section will be your best friend as you experiment on the grill. Mix and match your favorites with any recipe you choose—that's what they're here for. As always, marinate for a longer period of time in order to achieve a deeper flavor.

Easy Ginger Marinade

ACTIVE TIME: 5 MINUTES • TOTAL TIME: 5 MINUTES • SERVES 6

This marinade is perfect for chicken, but it really works with anything. If you're using meat, marinate for about 30 minutes; for vegetables, at least 15 minutes.

⅓ cup soy sauce

⅔ cup cooking wine

1 tablespoon sesame oil

1 clove garlic, minced

1 teaspoon ginger root, minced

1 teaspoon lime juice

¼ cup cilantro, chopped

In a small bowl, mix all of the ingredients together. Use the marinade to coat meat or veggies.

 GO PALEO! Use coconut aminos instead of soy sauce.

 GLUTEN-FREE! Instead of soy sauce, use coconut aminos or tamari to make this sauce gluten-free.

Teriyaki Marinade

This is a really simple teriyaki marinade I utilize constantly!

Mix all ingredients together and add to meat or vegetables. Marinate for a few hours in the refrigerator. Be sure to cook on low because of the high sugar content in this recipe.

½ cup soy sauce
½ cup ketchup
½ cup sugar
1 teaspoon ginger
1 teaspoon garlic powder

 GO PALEO! Use coconut aminos instead of soy sauce. Additionally, grab some paleo ketchup from the supermarket, make some using the recipe in our "Substitutions" chapter, or leave it out of this marinade.

 GLUTEN-FREE! Instead of soy sauce, use coconut aminos or tamari to make this sauce gluten-free.

Barbecue Rub

ACTIVE TIME: 5 MINUTES • TOTAL TIME: 5 MINUTES • SERVES 4-6

A simple rub can make all the difference when barbecuing something, whether it be half a zucchini or 10 ounces of steak. This one is particularly nice because it works with all diets.

1 teaspoon cumin

1 teaspoon paprika

1 teaspoon garlic powder

1 teaspoon onion powder

1 teaspoon chili powder

1 teaspoon salt

¼ teaspoon ground black pepper

Mix ingredients together in a small bowl!

 GLUTEN-FREE! Double check that the chili powder you're using was not produced with wheat.

Lemon Kebab Marinade

This tangy marinade works so well with a simple salad; imagine what it can do for your fresh garden greens.

½ cup olive oil

⅓ cup lemon juice

1–1½ teaspoons sugar

¼ teaspoon garlic powder

¼ teaspoon pepper

1 teaspoon salt (optional)

Whisk the ingredients together in a small bowl until evenly blended. Use this to marinate meat or vegetables!

Thai Peanut Sauce

ACTIVE TIME: 5 MINUTES • TOTAL TIME: 5 MINUTES • SERVES 6

This sauce is perfect for any dish needing some Thai flavor. It's easy to make and can save even the most boring dish from flavor purgatory.

3 tablespoons peanut butter, natural

3 tablespoons warm water

2 tablespoons soy sauce

2 teaspoons rice vinegar

2 teaspoons ginger, grated

1 teaspoon honey

½ teaspoon chili garlic sauce

1. Whisk together peanut butter, water, soy sauce and rice vinegar until the mixture is smooth.

2. Add in ginger, honey and chili garlic sauce and stir.

 MAKE IT VEGAN! Instead of honey, use agave nectar.

 GO PALEO! Use almond butter instead of peanut butter and use coconut aminos instead of soy sauce.

 GLUTEN-FREE! Instead of soy sauce, use coconut aminos or tamari to make this sauce gluten-free.

Balsamic Marinade

ACTIVE TIME: 5 MINUTES • TOTAL TIME: 5 MINUTES • SERVES 4

Acidic and just a little sweet, balsamic flavors pair so well with vegetables—especially if they've had time to marinate prior to being grilled or tossed. Try this with zucchini, tomatoes, eggplant or any salad you've thrown together.

3 tablespoons olive oil

2 tablespoons red wine vinegar

2 tablespoons lemon juice

1 tablespoon Dijon mustard

2 cloves garlic, minced

Pinch of salt and pepper

Mix the ingredients in a small bowl and use as a marinade on just about everything!

 GLUTEN-FREE! You can find gluten-free Dijon mustard at most supermarkets, but be warned: Some Dijons may not be gluten-free due to cross contamination during production.

Lemon Vinaigrette

ACTIVE TIME: 5 MINUTES • TOTAL TIME: 5 MINUTES • SERVES 1

A classic in any kitchen, this recipe serves as either a dressing or a marinade.

Mix all of the ingredients together in a small bowl and whisk until they've blended evenly.

3 tablespoons lemon juice

½ teaspoon Dijon mustard

¾ cup olive oil

Salt and pepper, to taste

1 sprig rosemary (optional, for garnish)

 GLUTEN-FREE! Don't forget: Some Dijon mustards may not be gluten-free due to cross contamination during production. Check with your grocer—or the Internet—if you aren't sure!

Strawberry Balsamic Vinaigrette

This sweet vinaigrette is perfect for a summer barbecue.

1 cup strawberries, de-stemmed

¼ cup balsamic vinegar

¼ cup olive oil

1 tablespoon Dijon mustard

1 clove garlic, minced

Salt and pepper, to taste

1. Preheat your grill to medium heat and place your de-stemmed strawberries on a large sheet of foil. Fold the foil over the strawberries to seal them in and create a foil pocket.

2. Making sure to keep all the juices in the foil, grill for 15–20 minutes or until the strawberries caramelize.

3. After they're fully cooked, remove and add all ingredients to a blender or food processor. Adding the juices from the grilled strawberries, puree until the mixture becomes smooth and serve cold.

 GLUTEN-FREE! Dijon alert! Remember to double check that your mustard is gluten-free before purchasing.

Spicy Orange Marinade

ACTIVE TIME: 5 MINUTES • TOTAL TIME: 5 MINUTES • SERVING SIZE: 1 CUP

Providing cooks with the ever-popular combination of sugar and spice, the orange and chili flavors play nicely off one another. Up the chili powder should you want a bit more heat.

2 tablespoons olive oil

1 tablespoon orange marmalade

1 tablespoon orange juice

1 tablespoon cilantro, chopped

½ teaspoon chili powder

Salt and pepper, to taste

Mix the ingredients in a small bowl. Marinate your meat or veggies for at least 30 minutes in the refrigerator.

Salads & Sides

This section is filled to the brim with my favorite salads and sides. Odds are, you haven't grilled the majority of your salad before—the method brings diverse and smoky flavors to dishes crying out for that extra bite, all while bringing out the natural flavors of the vegetables you intend to celebrate. These can also double as entrees depending on how many you're feeding and how many add-ons you want to incorporate.

Grilled Peach and Corn Salsa

ACTIVE TIME: 15 MINUTES • TOTAL TIME: 20 MINUTES • SERVES 6

The ultimate summer salsa, this smoky sweet treat works as a standalone dish. Instead of the usual chips and salsa, try this over a cup of rice or anything off the grill for something heartier.

3 medium peaches, peeled, pit removed and chopped

2 ears sweet corn

1 tablespoon olive oil

1 cup cherry or grape tomatoes, halved

⅓ cup red onion, diced

1 jalapeno, minced

¼ cup cilantro, chopped

1 large avocado, pit removed, diced

2 tablespoons lime juice

Salt and pepper, to taste

1. Preheat grill to medium heat. Brush olive oil onto ears of corn and grill for about 5 minutes, turning throughout. Remove from heat when grill marks appear.

2. Remove kernels from cob into a large bowl. Add chopped peaches, tomatoes, red onion, jalapeno and cilantro. Mix together and gently stir in the avocado pieces.

3. Add lime juice, salt and pepper. Stir gently and serve.

 ADD MEAT! Serve over grilled chicken. Grill 1 pound of skinless, boneless chicken breast over medium heat for 5–6 minutes per side or until it becomes tender.

 MAKE IT VEGAN! This recipe is already vegan, but for more substance serve it over 1 cup of cooked rice.

Grilled Zucchini Salsa

Salsa is better when it's interesting, and the best way to make it interesting is by introducing new flavors. The smokiness the zucchini brings makes this a standout.

1. In a medium bowl, combine the tomatoes, onions, and chili peppers, making sure to drain slightly. Stir in the vinegar and salt. Set your salsa aside.

2. Preheat grill to medium heat and prepare a piece of foil large enough to hold all of the zucchini rounds. Brush both sides of the zucchini slices lightly with oil and place them on the foil. Top each round with salsa and fold the foil around the zucchini. Crimp the edges and tightly seal the foil.

3. Place the packet on the grates and cook for 20–25 minutes or until the zucchini is tender.

4. Remove from heat and sprinkle with cheese.

2 small zucchini, cut into ½-inch rounds

1 tablespoon olive oil

6 large tomatoes, chopped

1 white onion, chopped

¾ cup green chili peppers, chopped

1 teaspoon vinegar

1 teaspoon salt

½ cup pepper jack cheese, shredded

 ADD MEAT! Serve this over steak or grilled chicken. I like it over chicken, so I use 1 pound of skinless, boneless chicken breast that's been grilled for 5–6 minutes on each side. Remove from heat when it is properly cooked through.

 MAKE IT VEGAN! Remove the cheese from this recipe or replace it with a substitute.

 GO PALEO! Remove the cheese or replace it with a substitute.

Corn Salsa

ACTIVE TIME: 5 MINUTES • TOTAL TIME: 10 MINUTES • SERVES 4

In my opinion, grilled corn improves any dish. And since you most likely aren't growing corn in your backyard or on your windowsill, working it into a salsa with some bite is a nice way to make it your own.

1. Preheat grill to medium-high heat. Place corn directly on the grill. Turn the corn and grill for about 8 minutes, or until corn becomes lightly charred and kernels have browned. Let these cool for a bit and then cut the kernels from the cob into a large bowl.

2. Place the tomatoes, red onions and pepper into a food processor and puree. Add mixture to the bowl of grilled corn and mix. Stir in the cilantro and serve.

1 ear corn, shucked
1 pint cherry tomatoes
½ diced red onion
1 serrano pepper
½ cup cilantro, chopped

 ADD MEAT! Serve this over grilled chicken. Grill 1 pound of skinless, boneless chicken breast over medium heat for 5–6 minutes per side. Serve the salsa over the chicken and enjoy.

 MAKE IT VEGAN! While the recipe is already vegan, you can add to the deliciousness by serving over brown or white rice.

Pineapple Salsa

This extra sweet salsa works whether hot or cold—just be sure the pineapple is fresh so as not to disturb the dish's balance.

¼ cup cilantro

½ pineapple, sliced

1 tablespoon lime juice

½ serrano pepper, diced

1 orange or yellow bell pepper, finely chopped

1 small sweet onion, finely chopped

Pinch of sugar

Pinch of salt and pepper

1. Preheat the grill to medium-high heat. Grill the pineapple slices until grill marks appear.

2. Dice pineapple on a cutting board and transfer pineapple cubes to a medium bowl. Mix together with cilantro, lime juice, chili pepper, bell pepper and onion. Season with sugar, salt, and pepper. Serve warm or cold. For cold, refrigerate for about an hour before serving.

 ADD MEAT!   Grill up 1 pound of skinless, boneless chicken over medium heat. Cook each side for 5–6 minutes each, or until chicken is fully cooked through. Serve the salsa over chicken and enjoy.

 MAKE IT VEGAN!   This recipe is already vegan, but serve it over 1 cup of cooked rice for a more substantial meal. Cook the rice according to package instructions and drizzle salsa on top.

 GLUTEN-FREE!   This recipe is already gluten-free, but for some extra flavor try mixing in one small, chopped jalapeno pepper as well.

Grilled Cabbage

ACTIVE TIME: 15 MINUTES • TOTAL TIME: 45 MINUTES • SERVES 4

The small ingredients list ensures that the cabbage—a lovely leafy green that receives far less fanfare than it deserves—will shine in the spotlight.

1. Preheat your grill to medium heat and cut the large head of cabbage into 8 wedges.

2. Remove the core and place the wedges on a piece of large aluminum foil. Season to taste using garlic powder, salt, and pepper.

3. Create a foil packet by folding the foil over and crimping the edges. Grill covered for 30-40 minutes, until tender. Remove from heat and serve.

1 large head of cabbage

1½ teaspoons garlic powder

Salt and pepper, to taste

 ADD MEAT! To add some extra flavor, cook up some bacon and brush the bacon grease on the cabbage before grilling. Serve with bacon strips.

Grilled Corn Guacamole

ACTIVE TIME: 10 MINUTES • **TOTAL TIME: 15 MINUTES** • **SERVES 4-6**

Guacamole is good no matter how it's made; this version utilizes grilled corn to add some extra sweetness. Serve this over any dish, use it as a dip or just eat it with a spoon.

1 ear of corn, shucked

3 avocados

¼ cup cilantro, chopped

¼ cup red onion, diced

2 serrano chilis, minced

2 tablespoons lime juice

¼ cup feta cheese

Salt and pepper, to taste

1. Preheat grill to medium-high heat. Grill corn, turning occasionally, until all sides have charred. This should take about 8 minutes. Once corn is sufficiently grilled, remove the kernels from the cob and set aside.

2. Cut the avocados in half and remove their pits. Using a spoon, scoop out the avocado flesh and transfer to a medium bowl.

3. Using a fork, mash the avocado until it reaches desired consistency. Add corn, cilantro, onion, serrano chilis, lime juice and feta. Mix these together until they reach desired consistency and add salt and pepper, to taste. Serve and enjoy.

 ADD MEAT! Serve this over grilled chicken. Grill 1 pound of skinless, boneless chicken until it has thoroughly cooked through, about 5–6 minutes on each side.

 MAKE IT VEGAN! Remove the feta cheese from the recipe.

 GO PALEO! Join our vegan friends and toss that feta cheese aside!

Grilled Sweet Onions

ACTIVE TIME: 15 MINUTES • TOTAL TIME: 45 MINUTES • SERVES 4

These onions are the perfect side for almost any meal, which this recipe often comes in handy in a pinch. As the onions can grill alongside whatever else you're cooking, don't be deterred by the total cooking time.

4 large sweet onions

4 cloves garlic, minced

¼ cup butter

1 teaspoon salt

1. Cut the onions into quarters and place them on a large piece of foil. Sprinkle the minced garlic over them and dot with butter.

2. Add a pinch of salt, fold the foil over and crimp the edges to seal and form a foil packet.

3. Preheat grill to medium heat and place the packet on the grates. Grill for about 30 minutes covered. Remove from heat and serve.

 ADD MEAT! Serve this with Paleo Pork Chops, found in the "Substitutions" section.

 MAKE IT VEGAN! Replace the butter with 3 tablespoon of olive oil.

 GO PALEO! This recipe is already paleo, but you can't go wrong serving it alongside the aforementioned Paleo Pork Chops.

Caramelized Corn

ACTIVE TIME: 15 MINUTES • TOTAL TIME: 20 MINUTES • SERVES 4

As good as grilled corn is, it's even better when it's caramelized.

1. Create your caramel sauce by mixing the ingredients (minus the corn) in a small bowl. Place to the side.

2. Preheat your grill to high and oil the grill grates. Place corn on grill and cook for about 5 minutes, turning regularly.

3. Keeping the corn on the grill, baste each ear in your caramel sauce and continue grilling for 5 more minutes. Make sure the corn becomes tender and slightly charred before taking it off the grill.

4 ears corn, husked

3 tablespoons brown sugar

1 teaspoon cayenne pepper

¼ cup butter, melted

Pinch of salt and ground pepper, to taste

 ADD MEAT! Since this is a side dish, you can add meat to it however you like. My favorite way is to transform this dish into a smoky corn salad by grilling and dicing up some flank steak. Grill 1½ pounds of flank steak for 5 minutes per side, removing from heat when it reaches desired doneness. Dice and mix it with corn removed from husks, then serve.

 MAKE IT VEGAN! Replace butter with 2 tablespoons of olive oil.

Spicy Grilled Corn

ACTIVE TIME: 10 MINUTES • TOTAL TIME: 20 MINUTES • SERVES 4

Transform your sweet grilled corn into something smoky, spicy and complex, simply by adding olive oil and a few select spices. I love serving this with beans or quinoa.

1. In a small bowl, mix all of the ingredients minus the olive oil and corn.

2. Brush the olive oil on the corn to help the coating stick.

3. Sprinkle the mixture over the corn and place each ear in a large piece of foil. Fold the foil over and crimp edges to create a tightly sealed packet.

4. Preheat grill to medium heat and cook for 10–12 minutes, making sure to turn the packet occasionally. When the corn is tender and charred, remove from heat and serve.

2 teaspoons cumin

2 teaspoons coriander

1 teaspoon salt

1 teaspoon rosemary, finely chopped

½ teaspoon ground ginger

¼ teaspoon pepper

¼ teaspoon cinnamon

2 tablespoons olive oil

4 ears of corn, shucked

 ADD MEAT! Prepare 1 pound of steak for grilling by brushing with olive oil and sprinkling with the spice mixture. Rub the mixture in and let it sit to make sure the steak is properly coated. Grill each side for about 6 minutes (rare) over medium heat, or until desired tenderness is reached. Slice and serve.

Yellow Squash

When your squash is finally ready for harvest, you could do a lot worse than throwing it on the grill and serving it with some protein-packed brown rice. Simple, elegant and delicious—this trusty recipe won't let you down.

1 cup brown rice

3 medium yellow squash

2 small zucchini

½ cup olive oil

2 cloves garlic, minced

Salt and pepper, to taste

1. Cook brown rice according to package instructions and set aside.

2. Preheat your grill to medium heat. Cut the squash and zucchini into strips, about ¹/₂-inch thick.

3. In a pan, heat the olive oil and minced garlic. Once the garlic starts to sizzle, remove from heat and set aside.

4. Brush the squash and zucchini with the heated oil and garlic and add salt and pepper.

5. Place the vegetables on the grill and cook until slight grill marks appear. This should take about 5 minutes per side. Remove from heat and serve over rice.

 ADD MEAT! Serve this with grilled lamb chops. In a small bowl, combine 1 minced shallot, 1 teaspoon of dried oregano, 1 teaspoon of black pepper, 1 teaspoon of salt, ¹/₄ cup of olive oil, 3 cloves of minced garlic and 2 tablespoons of lemon juice. Mix well and pour the marinade over 6 lamb chops in a large resealable bag. Toss to ensure even coating. Marinate in the refrigerator for at least 1 hour. Grill on high heat for 5–6 minutes per side, or until the lamb chops become tender.

 GO PALEO! Remove the brown rice and try the lamb chop recipe above!

 GLUTEN-FREE! Instead of brown rice, serve this over white rice.

Frozen Veggie Makeover

ACTIVE TIME: 10 MINUTES • TOTAL TIME: 20 MINUTES • SERVES 4

Everybody knows the issues that come with eating frozen vegetables. They're much easier to cook and store than fresh vegetables, but they simply don't taste the same. But with some help from a hot grill and a cabinet of herbs and spices, there's no reason to abandon the pre-packaged options.

1. Mix all of the ingredients together in a large bowl, tossing to coat the vegetables.

2. Prepare a large piece of tin foil to make a foil packet. Transfer the vegetables to the foil and fold it over, crimping edges to seal it tightly.

3. Preheat grill to medium heat and grill packet for 6–7 minutes on either side. Remove from heat when the vegetables are tender and serve.

3½ cups frozen mixed vegetables, thawed

1 tablespoon olive oil

1 teaspoon thyme

1 teaspoon oregano

1 teaspoon parsley

¼ teaspoon salt

ADD MEAT! Serve this with steak. Prepare the steak for grilling by brushing with olive oil and sprinkling with salt and pepper. Grill each side for about 6 minutes (rare) over medium heat, or until desired tenderness is achieved. Dice and add to the salad.

Grilled Peach Salad

ACTIVE TIME: 5 MINUTES • TOTAL TIME: 20 MINUTES • SERVES 4

This juicy, sweet salad pairs wonderfully with pork chops, if you're serving meat-eaters.

3 peaches, pitted and halved

2 bell peppers, sliced

2 tablespoons olive oil

1 tablespoon honey

4 cups baby arugula

3 tablespoons slivered almonds

½ tablespoon lemon juice

1. Preheat your grill to high heat and prepare the peaches by halving them and removing their pits.

2. Brush the cut side of each peach with olive oil and place directly on the grill, cut side down. Brush the bell pepper slices with oil and place them on the grill as well.

3. Grill the peaches for about 2–3 minutes, or until they become caramelized, and grill the bell peppers for about 8 minutes, flipping once.

4. Remove the peppers from heat when they have become tender. Flip the peaches after they've become caramelized and grill for another 2 minutes, just to heat them through.

5. Remove the peaches from the grill and slice them into bite-sized pieces. Dice the bell peppers after removing from heat.

6. In a large bowl, combine the peaches, peppers, arugula and slivered almonds and toss. Drizzle honey and lemon juice over the top, toss to coat and serve.

 ADD MEAT! Pair this with the Paleo Pork Chops in "Substitutions."

 MAKE IT VEGAN! Replace honey with agave nectar or coconut nectar.

Maple Smoked Vegetables

ACTIVE TIME: 20 MINUTES • TOTAL TIME: 45 MINUTES • SERVES 8

Maple syrup can be overpowering, but in this case the variety of vegetables is able to stand up to the incredible sweetness.

⅓ cup balsamic vinegar

⅓ cup maple syrup

1 large red onion

1 pound fresh asparagus, trimmed

2 medium zucchini

2 bell peppers

1 medium summer squash

2 tablespoons olive oil

1 teaspoon dried thyme

Salt and pepper, to taste

1. Start by making your maple glaze in a small saucepan. Place vinegar and syrup in the saucepan and bring this mixture to a boil. Reduce heat and cook until it thickens, which should take about 6–8 minutes. Remove from heat and set aside for later use.

2. Cut the onion, zucchini, bell pepper and summer squash into slices. Place the vegetables in a large bowl and toss to coat with olive oil and salt.

3. Preheat your grill to medium heat and lightly oil the grates. Arrange the vegetables on the grill and cook, covered, for 10 minutes on each side.

4. Brush half of the glaze on and grill for 5–8 more minutes, or until vegetables become tender. Remove from heat, brush on the remaining glaze and serve.

 ADD MEAT! Maple smoked ribs are the perfect match for this meal this meal. Double the glaze and brush it onto 1 rack of your favorite type of pork. You'll have to grill them for about 2 hours, but it's definitely worth it.

 MAKE IT VEGAN! Make sure to use all-natural maple syrup.

Soy Sauce Veggies

ACTIVE TIME: 10 MINUTES • TOTAL TIME: 20 MINUTES • SERVES 4

By now you've seen for yourself how well vegetables cook in these foil packets. These go incredibly well with chicken or even over rice. I love how the soy sauce bursts from these warm vegetables after they've been cooked together.

1. Prepare the veggies by cutting them into thin slices and placing them in a large mixing bowl. Toss with the butter and soy sauce.

2. Cut a large piece of foil to make a packet. Place the veggies on the foil and drizzle extra soy sauce over them. Fold and seal the packet, crimping the edges.

3. Preheat grill to medium heat and place the packet on the grill. Cook for 12–14 minutes, flipping halfway. Grill the veggies until they are tender, remove from heat and serve.

1 medium green pepper
1 medium red pepper
1 medium yellow pepper
2 medium zucchini
1 small summer squash
1 tablespoon butter, melted
2 teaspoon soy sauce

 ADD MEAT! Cook 1 pound of skinless, boneless chicken in the packet with the veggies. Cut it into 1-inch cubes and grill until the cubes reach desired tenderness.

 MAKE IT VEGAN! Replace butter with 2¼ teaspoons olive oil.

 GO PALEO! Use coconut aminos instead of soy sauce.

 GLUTEN-FREE! Instead of soy sauce, use coconut aminos or tamari to make this sauce gluten-free.

Lime and Sesame Vegetables

ACTIVE TIME: 10 MINUTES • TOTAL TIME: 20 MINUTES • SERVES 6

This is such a refreshing dish that I encourage you to repurpose it all year long. Something this tasty shouldn't be limited to just the summer time!

3 tablespoons lime juice

1 tablespoon sesame oil

1½ teaspoons soy sauce

1 clove garlic, minced

½ teaspoon fresh ginger, ground

Pinch of salt and pepper

1 medium eggplant, cut into ¼-inch rounds

1 medium zucchini, cut into ¼-inch rounds

1 small summer squash, cut into ¼-inch rounds

2 teaspoons honey

⅛ teaspoon crushed red pepper

1. In a small bowl, mix together the lime juice, sesame oil, soy sauce, garlic, ginger and a pinch of salt and pepper. Mix well and set aside.

2. Cut your vegetables into slices and brush the mixture onto both sides of every slice.

3. Preheat grill to medium heat and place the slices on lightly oiled grates (use skewers if you'd like). Grill covered for 4–6 minutes on each side, or until the vegetables become tender and have slight grill marks. Add honey and red pepper flakes to the remaining lime juice mixture and drizzle over the grilled vegetables. Serve and enjoy.

 ADD MEAT! Brush 1 pound of skinless, boneless chicken breast with the lime juice mixture. Grill over medium heat for 5–6 minutes per side, making sure it is fully cooked before removing. Slice and serve.

 MAKE IT VEGAN! Replace honey with agave nectar or coconut nectar.

 GO PALEO! Use coconut aminos instead of soy sauce.

 GLUTEN-FREE! Instead of soy sauce, use coconut aminos or tamari to make this sauce gluten-free.

Summer Vegetable Packet

ACTIVE TIME: 10 MINUTES • TOTAL TIME: 30 MINUTES • SERVES 4

Nutrient-rich and flavorful, this foil packet recipe is a great way to show off your summer harvest. Limited seasoning brings out the vegetables' natural flavors as they smoke.

4 ears corn, shucked

2 bell peppers, diced

2 zucchini, cut into ½-inch slices

½ red onion, diced

½ teaspoon oregano

½ teaspoon garlic powder

½ teaspoon basil

½ teaspoon parsley

Salt and pepper, to taste

4 tablespoons olive oil

Feta cheese, for sprinkling

1. Begin by removing kernels from the cob into a medium bowl. Add bell pepper, zucchini slices and diced onions and mix together.

2. Sprinkle oregano, garlic powder, basil, parsley and a pinch of salt and pepper over the vegetables, making sure to mix thoroughly. Add the olive oil and toss to coat evenly.

3. Prepare two large pieces of foil and distribute the vegetables evenly between the two. Fold the foil into a packet and crimp the edges to seal.

4. Preheat grill to medium-high heat and place the packets on the grill. Let these cook for 15–20 minutes. Once vegetables are tender, remove from heat, sprinkle feta over each packet and serve.

 ADD MEAT! Add 3 slices of bacon to crumble over the vegetables! Prepare the bacon before proceeding to prepare the rest of the recipe. While vegetables are grilling, crumble the bacon into a small bowl and set aside. Once vegetables have finished cooking, sprinkle the bacon over the packets.

 MAKE IT VEGAN! Remove the feta cheese completely or replace it with one of the substitute vegan cheeses.

 GO PALEO! Remove the feta cheese from the recipe.

Watermelon Goat Cheese Salad

Watermelon is a surprising grill favorite, and its smoky flavor will play nicely with the tangy goat cheese.

1. Begin by slicing watermelon into 1-inch-thick slices.

2. Preheat your grill to high heat and brush olive oil onto one side of each slice. Grill until they become seared (about 4 minutes).

3. Slice strawberries into slivers and set aside.

4. Mix together olive oil, lime juice and a pinch of salt. Slice cucumber and toss in the dressing with strawberries.

5. Cut seared watermelon into chunks and toss with the rest. Sprinkle goat cheese and serve.

1 seedless watermelon
1 pint small strawberries
1 medium-sized cucumber
2 tablespoons olive oil
2 teaspoons lime juice
1 cup crumbled goat cheese
Pinch of salt

 ADD MEAT! As most do, this salad goes great with steak. Rub 1 1/2 pounds of flank steak with brown sugar, garlic powder and chili powder. Grill for 5 minutes on each side, or until steak reaches desired doneness. Slice and serve with the salad.

 MAKE IT VEGAN! Unfortunately, goat cheese is not vegan. The salad is just as delicious without cheese, but the goat cheese can be swapped with Moxarella or Macadamia Ricotta from the "Substitutions" chapter.

 GO PALEO! If you can find goat cheese that is from grass-fed goats, it can be used in this salad! Otherwise, the salad is still great without cheese.

Grilled Carrots

ACTIVE TIME: 5 MINUTES • TOTAL TIME: 20 MINUTES • SERVES 4

As they're filled with antioxidants, you can't go wrong grilling carrots. This recipe brings a little extra flavor to this commonly boiled root vegetable. Serve over rice or quinoa for a fuller plate.

1. In a medium bowl, combine the soy sauce, olive oil, ginger, cider and garlic. Brush the mixture on the carrots, coating well.

2. Preheat your grill to medium heat and place the carrots on the grill grates. Grill for 15–20 minutes, making sure to baste them frequently with the soy sauce mixture. When the carrots are nice and tender, move from heat and serve.

¼ cup soy sauce

¼ cup olive oil

1 tablespoon ginger, minced

1 tablespoon cider vinegar

1 clove garlic, minced

1 pound large carrots, cut in half lengthwise

 ADD MEAT! Serve these smoky carrots with grass-fed flank steak. Prepare the steak for grilling by brushing with the same mixture as the carrots. Grill each side for about 6 minutes (rare) over medium heat, or until desired tenderness is reached. Dice and serve with your carrots.

 GO PALEO! Serve with grass-fed flank steak and use coconut aminos instead of soy sauce.

 GLUTEN-FREE! Instead of soy sauce, use coconut aminos or tamari to make this sauce gluten-free.

Grilled Dijon Veggies

ACTIVE TIME: 10 MINUTES   •   TOTAL TIME: 30 MINUTES   •   SERVES 6

If you love mustard, I recommend increasing the amount of Dijon you include in this recipe. Its sharp flavor profile pairs nicely with any fresh vegetable.

¼ cup olive oil

2 tablespoons red wine vinegar

½ teaspoon dried oregano

1 teaspoon Dijon mustard

1 clove garlic, minced

Pinch of salt and pepper

2 medium zucchini,
cut into ¼-inch rounds

1 medium summer squash,
cut into ¼-inch rounds

1 small red onion, cut into wedges

1 bell pepper, cut into 2-inch strips

5 cremini mushrooms

6 cherry tomatoes

1. In a small bowl, combine the oil, red wine vinegar, dried oregano, Dijon and garlic and mix well.

2. Place the vegetables in a large, resealable bag and toss to coat with the dressing. Let this stand for about 15 minutes in the refrigerator.

3. Preheat your grill to medium heat and place the vegetables on the grill rack. Cook until they become tender, about 10–12 minutes. Remove from heat and serve.

 ADD MEAT! If you have the time, serve these veggies with Paleo Pork Chops for a wholesome meal. For the recipe, head to the "Substitutions" section.

 GO PALEO! See above—Paleo Pork Chops are your friend.

Grilled Okra

Okra is great because it's high in nutrients and low in calories. A favorite in the South, okra helps with detoxification and possesses countless other benefits. Luckily for us, it's also delicious.

1 pound fresh okra

¼ cup melted butter

¼ cup Cajun seasoning

1. Preheat your grill for high heat and lightly oil the grate to prevent sticking.

2. Lay 5 or 6 pieces of okra side by side, alternating direction. Take a bamboo skewer and run it all the way through the okra. Brush with melted butter to coat and season with Cajun seasoning.

3. Place the skewers on the grill, about 1 inch apart. Grill on each side for about 2 minutes or until the okra is charred, and serve.

 ADD MEAT! Skewer 1-inch steak cubes and grill them until they reach desired doneness!

 MAKE IT VEGAN! Instead of melted butter, use 3 tablespoons of olive oil.

Grilled Broccoli and Cauliflower

ACTIVE TIME: 5 MINUTES • TOTAL TIME: 20 MINUTES • SERVES 2

As proven by the "Substitutions" section, cauliflower is one of the more dynamic vegetables one can use. This side goes well with rice, quinoa or even pasta.

1. In a large bowl, combine broccoli, cauliflower, and onion. Toss to coat with olive oil.

2. Add the garlic salt, paprika and pepper. Toss to coat again.

3. Place all vegetables on a large piece of foil and fold along the edges, crimp, and seal into a packet.

4. Preheat grill to medium heat. Grill covered for 10–15 minutes. Be sure to check that the vegetables have become tender. Remove from heat open foil packet, and serve.

1 cup broccoli florets

1 cup cauliflower

1 small red onion, cut into wedges

¼ cup olive oil

Pinch of garlic salt, paprika and pepper

 ADD MEAT! This can be served with steak as well. Prepare the steak for grilling by brushing with olive oil and sprinkling with salt and pepper. Grill each side for about 6 minutes (rare) over medium heat, or until desired tenderness. Dice or slice and serve.

 GLUTEN-FREE! This recipe is already gluten-free, but add some protein by serving it over quinoa.

Grilled Lemon-Artichoke Medley

ACTIVE TIME: 10 MINUTES • TOTAL TIME: 15 MINUTES • SERVES 4

The criminally underrated artichoke is brought to new heights when infused with the tangy smokiness of the grilled lemons.

12 baby artichokes, outer leaves removed and stems trimmed

2 medium sized eggplants, cut into ½-inch rounds

4 lemons, halved

½ cup olive oil

Salt and pepper, to taste

1. You can begin this process up to 2 days in advance. Cook the baby artichokes in boiling salted water in a large saucepan for about 8 minutes, or until tender. Cut the artichokes in half and pat dry. If made in advance, cover and chill.

2. Preheat grill to medium heat. Brush the cooked artichokes, eggplant and flesh sides of lemon with olive oil. Sprinkle with salt and pepper, to taste.

3. Grill the vegetables for about 2 minutes per side, or until tender and slightly charred. Lemons should be grilled flesh side down for about 2 minutes. Transfer vegetables to a serving platter and squeeze grilled lemon over the tops. Serve and enjoy!

 ADD MEAT! This dish goes wonderfully with the Paleo Pork Chops ("Substitutions")

 MAKE IT VEGAN! This recipe is already vegan, but serve over brown rice for extra nutrients.

 GO PALEO! This is already a paleo dish, but seriously, you should make the pork chops.

 GLUTEN-FREE! Serve over quinoa for extra protein.

Grilled Eggplant and Broccoli Salad

ACTIVE TIME: 15 MINUTES • TOTAL TIME: 25 MINUTES • SERVES 4

Alone, it's a delicious side dish, but with the addition of protein and different variations it makes a filling meal. Use whichever greens best suit your tastes.

2 heads of broccoli, florets separated

4 tablespoons of olive oil

1 eggplant, cut into 1-inch-thick slices

1 large red onion, cut into rounds

1 avocado

1 tablespoon red wine vinegar

1 teaspoon Dijon mustard

1 tablespoon chopped oregano leaves

3 cups of arugula

Honey, to taste

1 zested lemon

1 small handful of slivered almonds

1. Cook broccoli in a pot of boiling, salted water until tender, which should take about 2 minutes. Drain and let cool.

2. Pat broccoli dry and place into a large bowl.

3. Prepare grill for medium-high heat. Brush the broccoli, round red onions and sliced eggplant with olive oil. Season the broccoli with salt.

4. Grill the eggplant until it becomes soft, and the broccoli and onions until they have a slight char.

5. Remove from grill and let cool, tossing occasionally. Once cool, chop the eggplant into cubes and add them to a serving bowl with the avocado, broccoli and onions.

6. In a small bowl, make your dressing by whisking together the red wine vinegar, Dijon and oregano. Mix in honey and olive oil to taste.

7. Add arugula to the serving bowl and toss. Drizzle salad with dressing, tossing occasionally to ensure an even coating. Add the lemon zest and slivered almonds and serve.

ADD MEAT!   Add 1 pound of boneless chicken breast. Trim fat to prep for grilling. Grill for 5–6 minutes per side, or until juices run clear. Dice and add to the salad.

 GO VEGAN!   Check your Dijon to make sure it is vegan-friendly.

 GO PALEO!   This recipe is already paleo, but if you'd like some extra protein, grill up some grass-fed flank steak. Prep the steak for grilling. Marinate the steak for a minimum of 4 and maximum of 12 hours. Grill each side for about 6 minutes (rare), or until desired tenderness. Dice and add to the salad.

 GLUTEN-FREE!   This recipe is already gluten-free. But for a different flavor, substitute zucchini and red peppers for the eggplant. Grill until they reach desired tenderness.

Grilled Asparagus Spears

ACTIVE TIME: 5 MINUTES • TOTAL TIME: 15 MINUTES • SERVES 4

This bare-bones recipe could not be any easier, but works as a lovely addition to the table. If you're looking for a quick meal, pair this with a plate of quinoa.

Preheat grill to medium heat. Coat asparagus with olive oil and season with salt and pepper. Place the spears on the lightly oiled grate and cook for 2–3 minutes, or to desired tenderness.

1 bunch fresh asparagus spears
Pinch of salt and pepper
1 tablespoon olive oil

 ADD MEAT!   Add bacon by wrapping a strip of bacon around each oiled spear. Place on the grill and cook for 4–6 minutes per side, or until the bacon becomes crisp. If the bacon falls off, secure each end with toothpicks.

Tofu Summer Salad

ACTIVE TIME: 10 MINUTES • TOTAL TIME: 45 MINUTES • SERVES 4

Personally, I could eat goat cheese by the pound, so this salad is a nice excuse to do that while also enjoying some fresh fruit and greens. I love the way the goat cheese complements the arugula, but any other leafy green will be just as tasty.

3 cups arugula

15 ounces goat cheese

1 pint strawberries, de-stemmed

1 pound firm tofu

¼ cup slivered almonds

Strawberry Balsamic Vinaigrette (optional)

1. Drain your tofu by placing between paper towels and pressing out remaining liquids, or by placing a weight on top and letting the tofu drain for about 30 minutes. Once the tofu has properly drained, cut it into ¼-inch cubes.

2. Preheat the grill to medium-high heat and thread the cubes onto skewers for easier grilling. Lightly oil the surface of the grill and cook the cubes for about 10 to 15 minutes, or until the tofu becomes slightly browned.

3. While the tofu is cooking, make a balsamic dressing using the Strawberry Balsamic Vinaigrette recipe in the "Marinades & Sauces" section and prepare strawberries by slicing into appropriately sized slices.

4. Once the tofu is cooked, remove from the grill and let cool before adding to salad. Create your salad by mixing arugula, goat cheese and strawberries in a bowl. Add the tofu, drizzle on your balsamic and serve.

 ADD MEAT!   Grill 1 pound of skinless, boneless chicken over medium heat for 5–6 minutes per side.

 MAKE IT VEGAN!   Remove the goat cheese and replace with Moxarella cheese from the "Substitutions" chapter.

 GO PALEO!   Grill up some grass-fed flank steak. Prepare the steak for grilling by brushing with olive oil and sprinkling with salt and pepper. Grill each side for about 6 minutes (rare), or until desired tenderness. Dice and add to the salad.

Grilled Corn and Black Bean Salad

ACTIVE TIME: 15 MINUTES • TOTAL TIME: 20 MINUTES • SERVES 4

Black beans and corn is a classic combination, upon which you can add any greens you prefer.

1. Preheat grill to medium-high heat. Place four ears of corn directly on the grill. Grill for about 8 minutes, turning the corn regularly until it becomes lightly charred and the kernels have browned.

2. Let the ears cool for a bit, and cut the kernels off the cob into a large bowl.

3. Immediately mix in the lime juice and chili powder. Let the kernels fully cool, then mix in red pepper, cilantro leaves, spinach leaves, black beans and salt to taste.

4 ears of corn, husked

2 tablespoons lime juice

1 cup red peppers, finely chopped

½ cup cilantro leaves

½ cup fresh baby spinach leaves

1 can black beans, drained and rinsed

Pinch of chili powder

Pinch of salt

 ADD MEAT! Add 1 pound of 1¼-inch-thick New York strip steak. Brush the steak on both sides with olive oil and season generously with salt and pepper. Grill on medium heat for 4–5 minutes, turn over and cook for another 4–5 minutes for rare. Cook until the steak reaches desired tenderness, dice and add the cubes to the salad.

 GO PALEO! Unfortunately, black beans are not considered paleo. Remove the black beans but address your protein needs by adding steak, using the directions listed above.

Eggplant Salad

In my opinion, the insides of an eggplant make the perfect salad topping. But if you disagree, try substituting your favorite squash instead.

1 large eggplant

1 medium tomato, diced

1½ teaspoon red wine vinegar

½ teaspoon oregano

2 garlic cloves, diced

3 tablespoons olive oil

3 tablespoons parsley, chopped

Pinch of salt and pepper, to taste

1. Preheat grill to medium-high heat. Prick the eggplant with a fork, place on the grill and cook for about 15 minutes, covered. Cook until skin is soft, turning eggplant occasionally. Remove from heat and let cool.

2. Once the eggplant is cool, scoop out the insides and chop. Place this in a bowl and toss with diced tomatoes, vinegar, oregano, garlic and salt.

3. Add in the oil, parsley and pepper. Mix together and serve.

 ADD MEAT! This salad goes great with chicken. Grill chicken and serve diced in the salad or on the side.

Grilled Snap Peas and Mushrooms

ACTIVE TIME: 10 MINUTES • TOTAL TIME: 20 MINUTES • SERVES 6

These foil packet veggies are great with chicken or steak, or served over quinoa. Make these whenever you're short on time and energy but want something tasty and wholesome.

1. Prepare a large piece of foil to create a foil packet. Place the peas and mushrooms on the foil and sprinkle with onions and dill. Dot the sheet with butter, fold the foil tightly around the vegetables and crimp the edges to seal.

2. Preheat your grill to medium-high heat and grill the packet for 5 minutes.

3. Flip the packet over and cook for another 5–7 minutes. When the vegetables are tender, open the foil packet and allow steam to escape. Season with salt and pepper and serve.

1 pound sugar snap peas
½ cup cremini mushrooms, sliced
2 tablespoons green onions, sliced
1 teaspoon dill weed
2 tablespoons butter
Salt and pepper, to taste

 ADD MEAT! Serve with grilled chicken! Grill ½ pound of skinless, boneless chicken brushed with olive oil over medium heat. Grill until the chicken is fully cooked through, which should take 5–6 minutes per side. Serve sliced.

 MAKE IT VEGAN! Replace the butter with 1½ tablespoons of olive oil.

 GO PALEO! Serve with grass-fed flank steak. Prepare the steak for grilling by brushing with olive oil and sprinkling with salt and pepper. Grill each side for about 6 minutes (rare) over medium heat, or until desired tenderness. Dice and add to the salad.

Grilled Artichokes

ACTIVE TIME: 20 MINUTES   •   TOTAL TIME: 1 HOUR   •   SERVES 4

Any garden-lover will want to have a grilled artichoke recipe on hand, and honey and chili paste make for a unique twist on this classic concept.

4 medium artichokes

1 lemon

½ cup mayonnaise

1 tablespoon chili paste

1 tablespoon honey

Salt and pepper to taste

Olive oil

1. Prepare each artichoke by cutting off the top ½ inch and cutting down the middle lengthwise. Be sure to trim the pointed ends off of the leaves. Carefully remove the fuzzy choke in the center and discard.

2. Rub lemon over the artichoke halves. Add a steaming rack to a large pot, fill the pot with water and place the artichokes in the rack. Steam until they become tender, which should take between 30 and 40 minutes. Once they're tender, remove them from the rack and set aside to cool for about 15 minutes.

3. Preheat your grill to high heat. In a small bowl, combine mayonnaise, chili paste, honey and a pinch of pepper. Mix this well and set aside.

4. Brush the steamed artichokes with oil and sprinkle salt and pepper over them.

5. Grill the artichokes for about 4 to 5 minutes, cut side down. They should be slightly charred and ready to serve.

 ADD MEAT! Serve this with steak or chicken. Prepare steak or chicken for grilling by brushing with olive oil and sprinkling with salt and pepper. Grill each side for about 6 minutes (rare) over medium heat, or until desired doneness.

 MAKE IT VEGAN! Replace honey with agave nectar or coconut nectar. Replace mayonnaise with vegan mayo, found in most supermarkets.

 GO PALEO! Use the Paleo Mayonnaise recipe found in "Substitutions."

Corn and Tomato Salad

Perfect for a summer afternoon, this salad is a lovely marriage of tanginess and smokiness.

2 medium roma tomatoes, cut into ½-inch slices

2 ears corn, shucked

3 tablespoons olive oil

1 green onion, finely chopped

2 tablespoons parsley, minced

1 clove garlic, minced

1 teaspoon lemon juice

½ teaspoon lemon zest

¼ cup feta cheese, crumbled

3 cups baby spinach

Salt and pepper, to taste

1. Brush the tomatoes and corn with olive oil, sprinkling with salt and pepper. Preheat the grill to medium heat and place tomatoes and corn on the grill.

2. Cook tomatoes for 3–4 minutes, turning halfway, and remove from heat when slightly browned. Dice the tomatoes after they've cooled. Grill the corn for 10–12 minutes, turning occasionally. Remove from heat when corn is slightly charred.

3. Once corn has cooled, remove it from the cob by cutting it into a small bowl.

4. In the bowl, add green onion, parsley, garlic, lemon juice, lemon zest and a bit of olive oil. Mix this well and pour over diced tomatoes and baby spinach. Toss everything before sprinkling in the feta, plus any additional olive oil if necessary. Serve and enjoy.

 ADD MEAT! Serve this salad with grilled steak slices. Prepare the steak for grilling by brushing with olive oil and sprinkling with salt and pepper. Grill each side for about 6 minutes (rare) over medium heat, or until desired tenderness. Dice and add to the salad. Don't forget to drizzle it with the lemon dressing!

 MAKE IT VEGAN! Remove or replace the cheese from the recipe using your favorite from "Substitutions."

 GO PALEO! Remove the cheese or replace it, using paleo cheese from your local supermarket.

Italian Packet

Smoky Italian herbs pair beautifully with pasta for a more traditional, hearty meal.

1. In a small bowl, mix olive oil, butter, parsley, basil, oregano, garlic and salt.

2. Place the prepared vegetables on a large sheet of foil. Brush the mixture over each vegetable, making sure to fully coat the vegetables.

3. Fold the foil tightly around the vegetables to form a packet. Crimp the edges to seal and preheat your grill to medium heat.

4. Place the vegetable packet on the grill and cook for 15 minutes on each side, or until the vegetables become tender. Remove from heat and serve.

¼ cup olive oil

¼ cup butter

¼ cup parsley

1 teaspoon dried basil

½ teaspoon dried oregano

2 cloves garlic

Pinch of salt

1 medium zucchini, cut into ¼-inch rounds

1 medium eggplant, cut into ¼-inch rounds

2 medium bell peppers, cut into ¼-inch strips

½ pound cremini mushrooms

½ yellow onion, cubed

1 cup broccoli florets

1 cup cauliflower florets

 ADD MEAT! Serve these veggies with chicken. Slice 1 pound of skinless, boneless chicken into 1-inch cubes and add them to the foil packets. Cook until they reach desired doneness.

 MAKE IT VEGAN! Replace the butter with 3 tablespoons of olive oil.

Grilled Asparagus and Spinach Salad

ACTIVE TIME: 5 MINUTES • TOTAL TIME: 15 MINUTES • SERVES 4

This healthy salad is an easy recipe for anyone who likes asparagus. Enjoy the natural flavors of this recipe and feel free to add any other vegetables that you like.

1. Rinse asparagus and spinach and let it dry.

2. Remove stems from asparagus and toss with olive oil and balsamic vinegar in a large bowl. Add a pinch of salt and pepper.

3. Preheat your grill to medium-high heat. Grill asparagus for about 6 minutes, making sure to turn occasionally.

4. Remove from heat and chop before adding to a large bowl. Toss asparagus with spinach and cheese. Add any additional toppings and serve.

1 bunch asparagus
1 bunch spinach
1 tablespoon olive oil
2 tablespoons balsamic vinegar
Pinch of salt and pepper
¼ cup Parmesan cheese, grated

 ADD MEAT! Grill 1 pound of flank steak. Prepare the steak for grilling by brushing with olive oil and sprinkling with salt and pepper. Grill each side for about 6 minutes (rare), or until desired tenderness. Dice and add to the salad.

 MAKE IT VEGAN! Remove the cheese from this recipe and serve with the Vegan Parmesan alternative in "Substitutions," or no cheese at all!

 GO PALEO! Remove the cheese from the recipe and serve with flank steak.

Foil Pack Vegetables

ACTIVE TIME: 10 MINUTES • TOTAL TIME: 30 MINUTES • SERVES 4

There is no shortage of combinations you can try when making foil packet vegetables, but I love this one for its beautiful presentation; the vibrant colors make this dish look as good as it tastes.

1 small red onion, sliced

2 bell peppers, any color, sliced

1 cup green beans, cut

1 cup baby carrots

3 medium plum tomatoes, quartered

1 small zucchini, cut into ¼-inch rounds

3 tablespoons white vinegar

3 tablespoons olive oil

2 teaspoons dried oregano

Pinch of pepper

1. Prepare the vegetables by placing them on a thick, large piece of foil.

2. In a small bowl, mix together the vinegar, olive oil, oregano and a pinch of pepper. Brush mixture onto the vegetables until they are fully coated.

3. Fold the foil around the vegetables, forming a tight foil packet, and crimp and seal the edges.

4. Preheat your grill to medium heat and place the packet on the grates. Grill for 15–20 minutes or until the vegetables become tender. Open the foil and serve.

 ADD MEAT! Grill 1 pound of steak with this medley to add additional protein. Prepare the steak for grilling by brushing with the vinegar mixture. Grill each side for about 6 minutes (rare), or until desired tenderness. Slice and serve.

Green Bean and Arugula Salad

ACTIVE TIME: 10 MINUTES • TOTAL TIME: 25 MINUTES • SERVES 4

The bitter arugula serves as a perfect complement to the light, refreshing green beans in this easy salad.

1. Clean and trim green beans, then coat them with olive oil. Add salt and pepper to taste.

2. Preheat your grill to medium heat and coat the grates with oil. Spread the beans over the grate. Cover and cook for 15–20 minutes, making sure to rotate.

3. Once the beans are crispy and cooked through, remove them and toss with arugula, vinegar and chopped bell pepper.

1 bunch fresh green beans
1 tablespoon olive oil
1 bunch arugula
1 red bell pepper, chopped
2 tablespoons balsamic vinegar
Pinch of salt and pepper

 ADD MEAT! Prepare 1¼ pounds of skirt steak by seasoning with salt and pepper. Grill this for 5 minutes per side, or until it reaches desired doneness. Serve in slices over the salad.

Quinoa Salad with Grilled Veggies

ACTIVE TIME: 30 MINUTES • TOTAL TIME: 1 HOUR 20 MINUTES • SERVES 5

Quinoa is high in protein and better for you than most grains, ensuring that this hearty salad will keep everyone happy and healthy.

1 large red onion

2 large bell peppers, any color

1 medium zucchini

1 medium eggplant

1 pound asparagus spears

½ cup olive oil

2 tablespoons balsamic vinegar

1 clove garlic, minced

1 teaspoon thyme, dried

Salt and pepper, to taste

2 ears of corn, shucked

3 cups quinoa, cooked according to package instructions

2 tablespoons parsley, chopped

1 tablespoon mint, chopped

Lemon juice

Strawberry Balsamic Vinaigrette (optional)

1. Begin by slicing the onion, peppers, zucchini, eggplant and asparagus into approximately same-sized pieces.

2. Combine slices in a large bowl and drizzle them with balsamic vinegar and olive oil. Add garlic, thyme and a pinch of salt and pepper, and then toss to coat evenly. Let vegetables marinate for 1 hour.

3. Preheat your grill to medium heat. Spread the tossed vegetables across a large sheet of foil, cover with another sheet and crimp the edges, creating a sealed packet.

4. Let the packet cook for about 15–20 minutes or until vegetables become tender. Cutting the slices to approximately the same sizes will help ensure similar cooking times.

5. While your packet cooks, brush the ears of corn with olive oil and place them directly on the grill. Turn the corn and grill for about 8 minutes, or until corn becomes lightly charred and kernels have browned. Once the corn is properly tender, remove from heat and set aside to cool.

6. Add cooked quinoa to a large serving bowl. Once the corn is cool, cut the kernels from the cob and add to the serving bowl. Additionally, add the parsley and mint. Once your veggie packet has been properly cooked, remove from heat and chop the vegetables into bite-sized pieces, adding to the serving bowl.

7. Toss the salad and drizzle olive oil and some lemon juice. Finish it off with a pinch of salt and pepper and serve with dressing of your choosing. I recommend the Balsamic!

 ADD MEAT! Add 1 pound of boneless chicken to the grill. Prepare the chicken by trimming off any extra fat and rinse them. Grilling should take about 5 to 6 minutes per side. Remove when fully cooked, dice and add to the salad.

 GO PALEO! Assemble this salad without the quinoa. Serve it over 1 or 2 cups of fresh baby spinach leaves.

Grilled Portobello Salad

ACTIVE TIME: 15 MINUTES • TOTAL TIME: 20 MINUTES • SERVES 4

When you introduce the grill, every salad improves, and no recipe exemplifies that concept better than one with grilled portobellos. Enjoy this Italian-style salad in any season.

1. In a small bowl, mix together tomatoes, mozzarella, basil leaves, olive oil, garlic, salt and pepper. Place to the side and let sit.

2. Remove the stems and gills from mushrooms and lightly brush with oil.

3. Grill the mushrooms covered for 6–8 minutes per side, or until the caps become tender.

4. Remove from heat and dice the mushrooms.

5. In a large bowl toss the tomato mixture, salad greens and diced mushrooms, and serve.

4 large portobello mushrooms
2 cups grape tomatoes, halved
3 ounces fresh mozzarella, cubed
6 fresh basil leaves, torn
2 teaspoons olive oil
2 cloves garlic, minced
2 cups salad greens
Salt and pepper, to taste

 ADD MEAT! Grill steak to serve over or beside the salad. Marinate the steak in any way you like and grill each side for about 6 minutes, or until it reaches desired doneness.

 MAKE IT VEGAN! Replace mozzarella with Moxarella from "Substitutions!"

 GO PALEO! Remove mozzarella from the recipe completely, and add bite-sized chunks of grass-fed flank steak, cooked according to the directions listed above.

Squash Summer Salad

ACTIVE TIME: 15 MINUTES • TOTAL TIME: 25 MINUTES • SERVES 4

Fresh vegetables and a light, crisp dressing make this a perfect summer dish.

3 cups baby spinach

1 pound summer squash, your choosing

1 large zucchini

½ cup cherry tomatoes, cut in half

⅓ cup feta, crumbled

6 basil leaves

3 mint leaves

1 tablespoon Dijon mustard

¼ cup olive oil

⅛ cup balsamic vinegar

⅛ cup red wine vinegar

1. Preheat your grill to medium-high heat. In a small bowl, begin making the dressing by mixing together Dijon mustard, olive oil, balsamic vinegar and red wine vinegar. Mix together until it has blended evenly.

2. Cut the summer squash and zucchini into ½-inch pieces and brush with olive oil.

3. Grill your squash and zucchini for 6–8 minutes, turning once. Remove from heat once grill marks are present and the vegetables are tender.

4. Cut the vegetables into small cubes, brush with some of the dressing and set aside.

5. In a large serving bowl, mix together the baby spinach, grilled squash, cherry tomatoes, basil leaves and mint leaves. Toss with desired amount of dressing and feta cheese and serve.

 ADD MEAT! Grill 1 pound of flank steak over medium heat for 6 minutes per side, or until it reaches desired doneness.

 MAKE IT VEGAN! Remove the cheese from this recipe to make it vegan.

 GO PALEO! No feta for you.

 GLUTEN-FREE! Just double check that the Dijon mustard you use is gluten-free!

Balsamic Mixed Vegetable Salad

**ACTIVE TIME: 15 MINUTES • TOTAL TIME: 2 HOURS 25 MINUTES
(INCLUDES MARINATING TIME) • SERVES 6**

This is an easy favorite of mine that can be adjusted in several ways. All of the veggies can be swapped out for your favorites, and instead of baby spinach leaves you can use any other salad green you prefer.

1. Set the baby spinach aside and prepare vegetables by cutting them as described in "Ingredients."

2. In a large plastic bag or large, sealable bowl, mix the marinade ingredients together. Add the vegetables to the bag and seal it. Marinate the vegetables in the refrigerator for 2 hours. Turn or shake the vegetables occasionally for an even coat.

3. When you're ready to begin cooking, preheat the grill to high heat. Grill the vegetables for approximately 6 minutes on each side, or until slight grill marks appear and they become tender.

4. Rinse and dry the spinach and add it to a large serving bowl. Once the vegetables are properly cooked, add them to the large serving bowl and toss.

MARINADE

2 tablespoons olive oil

2 tablespoons parsley, chopped

2 tablespoons oregano, chopped

2 tablespoons basil leaves, chopped

1 tablespoon balsamic vinegar

1 teaspoon salt

½ teaspoon pepper, ground

6 cloves garlic, minced

VEGETABLES

1 red onion, cut into wedges

12 white button mushrooms

1 large eggplant, cut into ¼-inch rounds

1 medium zucchini, cut into ¼-inch rounds

2 bell peppers, cut into wedges

1 summer squash, cut into ¼-inch rounds

5 cups baby spinach

 ADD MEAT! Serve this with 1 pound of steak marinated the same way as the vegetables. This should also cook for about 5–6 minutes per side, or until steak has reached desired doneness.

 GO PALEO! Make sure you use grass-fed beef.

Lemon Asparagus Salad

This salad is heavily asparagus-based, but it's just as easy to substitute the spears out for any other vegetable you prefer.

¼ cup olive oil

¼ cup lemon juice

1 bunch asparagus spears

⅛ cup Parmesan cheese, grated

6 cups spring greens salad mix

1 tablespoon Parmesan-seasoned almond slices

1 cup cherry tomatoes

1 pinch salt and pepper

1. Preheat grill to low heat. In a bowl, combine asparagus, lemon juice and oil and toss to coat asparagus.

2. Grill the asparagus spears for about 5 minutes, making sure to turn while they're cooking. Remove from heat once tender.

3. In a large serving bowl, combine the spring greens, Parmesan cheese, almond slices, cherry tomatoes, salt and pepper.

4. Slice the asparagus into bite-sized pieces and add them to the salad with the lemon juice and olive oil. Toss the salad and serve.

 ADD MEAT! Crumbled bacon and torn slices of ham make great additions to this salad.

 MAKE IT VEGAN! Replace the Parmesan cheese with Vegan Parmesan Cheese from the "Substitutions" chapter. Additionally, use regular slivered almonds instead of Parmesan-seasoned almonds.

 GO PALEO! Remove the cheese completely from the recipe.

Grilled Watermelon Mozzarella Salad

ACTIVE TIME: 10 MINUTES • TOTAL TIME: 30 MINUTES • SERVES 4

I love grilling fruit just as much as vegetables. Watching it caramelize as it smokes gives me legitimate joy, and after you try this recipe I suspect it will for you too.

1. Preheat your grill to medium heat. Brush watermelon on both sides with olive oil, sprinkle salt and pepper and drizzle honey on both sides.

2. Place the watermelon on the grill and let cook for about 4 minutes, flipping once.

3. Remove from heat and slice the watermelon into bite-sized pieces.

4. Toss cherry tomatoes, arugula, mozzarella and basil leaves together. Add the watermelon and enjoy! Drizzle on some Balsamic Marinade ("Marinades & Sauces") if desired.

2 large watermelon slices
2 tablespoons olive oil
2 tablespoons honey
1 pint cherry tomatoes, halved
5 ounces fresh mozzarella
10 basil leaves
1 cup arugula
Balsamic Marinade (optional)
Salt and pepper, to taste

 ADD MEAT! Serve this with pork chops, using the directions in the paleo section below.

 MAKE IT VEGAN! Replace the mozzarella with Moxarella from the "Substitutions" chapter. Replace honey with agave nectar or coconut nectar.

 GO PALEO! Remove the cheese and serve this with Paleo Pork Chops "Substitutions".

Grilled Beet Salad

ACTIVE TIME: 15 MINUTES • TOTAL TIME: 45 MINUTES • SERVES 4

Nothing beats beets from the garden! A personal favorite of mine, beets are incredibly high in vitamin C, fiber, potassium and a slew of other essential vitamins.

6 beets, scrubbed and peeled
(can be red or golden, your choice)

2 tablespoons olive oil

2–3 ounces arugula

2–3 ounces baby spinach

½ cup goat cheese, crumbled

¼ cup slivered almonds

1 tablespoons Dijon mustard

¼ cup olive oil

⅛ cup balsamic vinegar

⅛ cup red wine vinegar

Salt and pepper, to taste

1. Preheat your grill to high heat. In order to create a packet for the grill, cut two large pieces of aluminum foil.

2. In a medium bowl, toss your cleaned beets with olive oil until coated evenly. Season with salt and pepper, to taste.

3. Place beets on foil, fold over edges, crimp to seal and form your foil packet. Place the packet on grill and cook for 30 minutes or until beets are tender. Remove from heat and let cool for about 5 minutes.

4. Mix together Dijon mustard, olive oil, balsamic vinegar and red wine vinegar in a small bowl, then set aside.

5. By now, your beets should have cooled—slice them into wedges and move them into a large serving bowl. Combine with arugula, baby spinach, goat cheese and slivered almonds. Drizzle your dressing over the salad and serve.

 ADD MEAT! Cook a few slices of ham until they've reached desired warmth and crispiness, tear them and crumble them over your salad.

 MAKE IT VEGAN! Remove the cheese from the salad.

 GO PALEO! Remove the cheese from the salad and add meat.

Grilled Artichoke Kale Salad

ACTIVE TIME: 10 MINUTES • TOTAL TIME: 25 MINUTES • SERVES 4

For more protein, and a more filling plate, non-paleo eaters can mix in some quinoa.

2 pounds Jerusalem artichokes, chopped

2 parsnips, chopped

2 bell peppers, chopped

1 cup baby bella mushrooms, chopped

5 cloves garlic, chopped

1 teaspoon salt

½ teaspoon ground black pepper

1–2 tablespoons vegetable oil

2 cups kale, rinsed

1. In a large bowl, toss the artichokes, parsnips, bell peppers and mushrooms with garlic, oil, salt and pepper. Toss to coat completely.

2. Prepare a large sheet of tin foil to make a packet. Place the coated vegetables on the foil, fold and crimp the edges to form a sealed packet.

3. Preheat grill to high heat and place the packet seam side up on the grill. Cook for 20–25 minutes or until the vegetables become tender.

4. Once they reached desired tenderness, remove from heat and toss in a large bowl with the kale. Serve and enjoy.

 ADD MEAT! Add strips of skirt steak to your salad. Prepare 1¼ pounds of skirt steak by seasoning with salt and pepper and grilling for 5 minutes per side, or until steak reaches desired doneness.

Tofu Broccoli Salad

ACTIVE TIME: 10 MINUTES • TOTAL TIME: 30 MINUTES • SERVES 4

This simple teriyaki salad is really tasty and filled with protein. It goes great with steak or quinoa—or both. Serve this salad for any meal and enjoy.

1. Cut the tofu block into chunks and remove excess water.

2. Use the Teriyaki Marinade recipe to marinate the tofu chunks for at least 15 minutes.

3. Grill tofu over medium heat for 10–15 minutes, turning occasionally. Remove from grill and set aside.

4. Brush the broccoli with the marinade mixture and grill until florets become tender, turning occasionally. This should take about 7–8 minutes.

5. When everything has finished grilling, toss with arugula, spinach, chickpeas and serve.

1 block of extra firm tofu, drained and pressed

1 head broccoli

1 tablespoon olive oil

Teriyaki Marinade ("Marinades & Sauces")

3 cups arugula

3 cups baby spinach

1 (15-ounce) can chickpeas

 ADD MEAT! When in doubt, make steak. For maximum flavor, marinate the steak in your Teriyaki Marinade for at least 1 hour in the refrigerator. Otherwise prepare the steak by brushing with olive oil and sprinkling with salt and pepper. Grill each side for about 6 minutes (rare) over medium heat, or until desired tenderness. Dice and add to the salad.

 GO PALEO! Remove the chickpeas and serve with grass-fed flank steak.

Sweet Onion Salad

ACTIVE TIME: 20 MINUTES • TOTAL TIME: 25 MINUTES • SERVES 4

Onion-lovers will want to memorize this recipe, which works in any season and utilizes the classic combination of balsamic, tomato and basil to bring out the onions' natural sweetness.

2 medium sweet onions

2 tablespoons olive oil

1 pint grape tomatoes

12–14 fresh basil leaves

2 teaspoons balsamic vinegar

1. Begin by peeling your sweet onions and cutting crosswise to about ½-inch thickness.

2. Halve the grape tomatoes and tear or thinly slice the basil leaves.

3. Preheat your grill to medium. You can either lay the onions directly onto the grill, or use skewers to help in turning them over. Brush the olive oil onto both sides of the onions and season with salt and pepper. Turn the onions at least once while grilling and cook for about 10 minutes, or until the edges become slightly soft and begin to char.

4. Remove from heat and cut the onions in half. Add them to a bowl and toss to separate the layers.

5. Add the tomatoes, basil, olive oil and vinegar and toss to get an even coating.

 ADD MEAT! Start by cutting ¾ pound of boneless, skinless chicken into relatively small cubes, about 1 inch in size. Thread these onto separate skewers and grill for 5–6 minutes, or until meat is no longer pink. Be sure to check for desired tenderness while grilling. Add these to the large bowl and toss with the rest of the salad.

Grilled Fruit Medley

ACTIVE TIME: 5 MINUTES • TOTAL TIME: 15 MINUTES • SERVES 4

If you have a fruit garden, I recommend using whatever you have on hand. As wonderfully as these nectary treats mix, nothing beats the freshness of homegrown produce.

1. Prepare by slicing the pineapple, orange and apple into ½-inch-thick slices and cutting the rest of the fruits in half.

2. In a large bowl, combine the oil, ginger, salt and 2 tablespoons of lemon juice.

3. Mix well and brush over the fruit, or toss in the large bowl.

4. Preheat your grill to medium-high heat and place fruit on coated grates. Grill for 2–4 minutes per side, or until fruit becomes tender.

5. Remove from heat and toss in a large serving bowl. Drizzle the remaining lemon juice over the grilled fruits and serve.

1 peeled and cored pineapple

1 navel orange

1 green apple

2 peaches

1 nectarine

2 plums

2 apricots

¼ cup olive oil

1 tablespoon fresh ginger, grated

Salt, to taste

4 tablespoons lemon juice

 ADD MEAT! Pair this recipe with lamb chops. Prepare your chops by combining 1 minced shallot, 1 teaspoon of dried oregano, 1 teaspoon of black pepper, 1 teaspoon of salt, ¼ cup of olive oil, 3 cloves of minced garlic and 2 tablespoons of lemon juice in a small bowl. Mix well and pour the marinade over 6 lamb chops in a large resealable bag. Toss to ensure even coating. Marinate in the refrigerator for at least 1 hour. Grill on high heat for 5–6 minutes per side, or until the lamb chops become tender.

 GO PALEO! The lamb chop recipe listed above is paleo as well.

Grilled Asparagus Salad

This recipe proves once again that fresh vegetables and a little cheese are all you need to make a great dish.

¼ cup olive oil

⅛ cup lemon juice

15 fresh asparagus spears

4 cups broccoli spears

3 cups baby spinach

3 cups arugula

⅛ cup grated Romano cheese

Salt and pepper, to taste

1. Preheat your grill to medium-low heat. In a small bowl, combine olive oil and lemon juice. Toss asparagus and broccoli to coat, adding a pinch of salt and pepper.

2. Place the asparagus and broccoli on the grill. Turning occasionally, cook asparagus for 5 minutes and broccoli for 6–8 minutes or until they become tender.

3. Remove from heat and chop asparagus into bite-sized pieces and toss in a large bowl.

4. Add the grilled broccoli, baby spinach, arugula and lemon-oil mixture from the bowl. Toss and serve.

 ADD MEAT! Grill 1 pound of skinless, boneless chicken breast over medium heat for 5–6 minutes per side, or until it has cooked through. Remove from heat, dice and add it to the salad.

 MAKE IT VEGAN! Remove the cheese from this recipe.

 GO PALEO! Remove the cheese from this recipe.

Grilled Romaine Salad

ACTIVE TIME: 5 MINUTES • TOTAL TIME: 10 MINUTES • SERVES 4

Grilled romaine may feel a bit uninspired, but the common leafy green provides a nice crunch alongside the steak seasoning flavors. Serve this with grains or meat.

1. Toss romaine lettuce with olive oil and season with steak seasoning.

2. Preheat your grill for medium heat. Oil the grates lightly to prevent sticking. Place the lettuce directly on the grill cut side down and cook for about 5 minutes. The lettuce is done cooking when it becomes slightly wilted and lightly charred.

3. Remove from heat, drizzle with lemon juice and sprinkle Parmesan cheese on top. Serve and enjoy!

1 tablespoon olive oil

1 head romaine lettuce, cut in half lengthwise

1 tablespoon steak seasoning

2 tablespoons lemon juice

Parmesan cheese, for sprinkling

 ADD MEAT! Prepare 1 pound of flank steak for grilling by brushing with olive oil and sprinkling with steak seasoning, salt and pepper. Grill each side for about 6 minutes (rare) over medium heat, or until desired tenderness. Dice and enjoy alongside your charred lettuce.

 MAKE IT VEGAN! Replace the cheese with one of the vegan cheese options in the "Substitutions" chapter, or remove it entirely.

 GO PALEO! Remove the cheese—the recipe is still just as delicious, I promise.

 GLUTEN-FREE! Be sure to check that the steak seasoning you're using is gluten-free, if it isn't, many supermarkets sell gluten-free steak seasoning!

Grilled Brussels Sprouts

ACTIVE TIME: 10 MINUTES • TOTAL TIME: 20 MINUTES • SERVES 4

Brussels sprouts are commonly served with bacon, but the smokiness from the grill more than makes up for the absence of pork in this dish.

1. Preheat your grill to medium-high heat. Lightly oil the grate to prevent sticking.

2. In a medium bowl, mix together melted butter, garlic, black pepper and a pinch of salt. Brush this mixture over the halved brussels sprouts.

3. Place sprouts on the grill and cook for about 10 minutes, or until tender with slight grill marks. Remove from heat, squeeze lime juice over the sprouts and serve.

2 tablespoons melted butter
16 ounces brussels sprouts, halved
1 clove garlic, minced
2 teaspoons black pepper
Salt, to taste
1 lime, halved

 ADD MEAT! For a simple addition, add 1 pound of skirt steak. Prepare the steak for grilling by brushing with olive oil and sprinkling with salt and pepper. Grill each side for about 6 minutes (rare) over medium heat, or until desired tenderness. Serve with brussels sprouts.

 MAKE IT VEGAN! Replace the butter with 5 teaspoons of olive oil.

 GO PALEO! Add grass-fed flank steak, prepare as listed in the "Add Meat" variation.

Mushroom and Asparagus Salad

ACTIVE TIME: 15 MINUTES • TOTAL TIME: 25 MINUTES • SERVING SIZE: 4

Mushrooms and asparagus coated in balsamic make a really delicious salad. You can add any other vegetables that you like, but I think these two play especially well together.

8 baby portobello mushrooms, stems removed

1 bunch asparagus

1 bell pepper, sliced

4 cups baby spinach

1 teaspoon balsamic vinegar

2 tablespoons olive oil

2 cloves garlic, minced

2 teaspoons lemon juice

1 teaspoon Dijon mustard

1. In a small bowl, mix balsamic vinegar, olive oil, garlic, lemon juice and mustard. Keep some of this dressing to the side.

2. Preheat your grill to high heat. In a large bowl, toss the dressing, mushrooms, asparagus and bell pepper slices. Let stand for 15 minutes to allow the dressing to soak in.

3. Place the mushrooms, asparagus and peppers on the grill and cook until tender and slightly charred. Grill asparagus for 5 minutes, turning occasionally. Grill mushrooms gill side down for 4 minutes, flip and grill for another 7 minutes. Grill bell pepper slices for 5–6 minutes per side.

4. Remove everything from heat, dice and toss in a large bowl with the remaining dressing and baby spinach. Serve and enjoy.

 ADD MEAT! Grill 1 pound of skirt steak marinated the same way as the mushrooms and asparagus. Grill over medium heat for about 6 minutes per side, or until meat reaches desired doneness.

Cajun Grilled Vegetable Bowl

ACTIVE TIME: 10 MINUTES • TOTAL TIME: 25 MINUTES • SERVES 4

This recipe will require the use of a grill basket or grill wok. If neither are available to you, you can use a disposable foil pan—just be sure to poke holes in the bottom to let the liquid drain. These Cajun grilled veggies are an easy dinner with some kick.

1. Prepare vegetables and place them into your grill basket or foil pan. Preheat your grill to medium heat.

2. Drizzle olive oil over the vegetables and grill uncovered for 8–12 minutes.

3. Remove from heat when the vegetables are tender and transfer them to a large bowl. Sprinkle with Cajun seasoning and toss to coat. Serve and enjoy.

1 medium summer squash, sliced

1 medium zucchini, sliced

1 medium tomato, sliced

1½ cups sliced mushrooms

1 medium white onion, sliced and separated into rings

¼ cup carrots, sliced

1 small eggplant, sliced

1 teaspoon Cajun seasoning

1 tablespoon olive oil

 ADD MEAT! This Cajun seasoning goes wonderfully on steak. Prepare the steak for grilling by brushing with olive oil and sprinkling with seasoning, salt, and pepper. Grill each side for about 6 minutes (rare) over medium heat, or until desired tenderness. Dice and add to the bowl.

Grilled Cauliflower Salad

ACTIVE TIME: 20 MINUTES • TOTAL TIME: 30 MINUTES • SERVES 4

As you know, I think of cauliflower as a hidden gem. But I especially love it in this salad, tossed with avocado and a great dressing!

½ cup uncooked Kamut berries

3 tablespoons olive oil

4 cups of cauliflower florets

2 tablespoons tahini

2 tablespoons lemon juice

2 tablespoons warm water

1 clove garlic, minced

2 cups baby arugula

1 avocado, thinly sliced

Salt and pepper, to taste

1. Cook Kamut according to package directions, rinse with cold water and drain.

2. Toss cauliflower in 1 tablespoon of olive oil to coat.

3. Place the cauliflower on a large piece of foil and fold along the edges, crimp and seal into a packet.

4. Preheat grill to medium heat and grill the packet for 10–15 minutes, covered. Be sure to check that the cauliflower have become tender before removing from heat to cool.

5. In a large bowl, mix 2 tablespoons of olive oil, tahini, lemon juice, water, minced garlic and a pinch of salt and pepper. Mix evenly and then toss the grilled cauliflower with 1 tablespoon of your dressing.

6. Add arugula and Kamut to the large bowl and toss to coat.

7. Divide the cauliflower and avocado slices evenly and serve with your Kamut mixture.

 ADD MEAT! Cook 1 pound of skinless, boneless chicken over medium heat for 5–6 minutes per side. Serve over your salad.

 GLUTEN-FREE! Double check that the tahini you buy says "gluten-free." Additionally, remove the Kamut berries from the recipe.

Kale and Tomato Salad

This nutrient-rich salad is guaranteed to leave you full and satisfied and couldn't be easier to make.

1. Cook the quinoa according to package instructions. Let this stand while you grill the vegetables.

2. Brush the tomatoes, zucchini and kale with olive oil and preheat your grill to medium heat.

3. Grill the tomatoes and zucchini for 5–6 minutes, turning occasionally. Grill the kale for about 2 minutes.

4. Once fully cooked, remove from heat and toss with vinaigrette, baby spinach and quinoa. Serve and enjoy.

1 pint cherry tomatoes

1 zucchini, cut into ¼-inch rounds

1 bunch of kale

2 cups baby spinach

1 bell pepper, sliced

Strawberry vinaigrette ("Marinades & Sauces")

1 tablespoon olive oil

½ cup quinoa, cooked

 ADD MEAT! Add strips of steak to this salad to add some protein. Prepare the steak for grilling by brushing with olive oil and sprinkling with salt and pepper. Grill each side for about 6 minutes (rare) over medium heat, or until desired tenderness. Dice and add this to the salad.

 GO PALEO! Replace the quinoa with Cauliflower Rice from "Substitutions," or remove it completely.

Basil Vinaigrette Salad

ACTIVE TIME: 20 MINUTES • TOTAL TIME: 30 MINUTES • SERVES 4

This is a pretty simple salad with a delicious basil vinaigrette. It can be easily adjusted to fit vegan and paleo diets, as it's already gluten-free. I love serving this with chopped grilled chicken as well.

½ cup olive oil

¼ cup balsamic vinegar

1 teaspoon red wine vinegar

3 tablespoons fresh basil, minced

1 teaspoon chopped shallot

1 teaspoon rosemary

1 teaspoon lemon juice

Pinch of salt and pepper

2 ears corn, shucked

1 teaspoon olive oil

6 cups baby spinach

12 cherry tomatoes, halved

¼ cup slivered almonds

5 ounces goat cheese, crumbled

1. Make the dressing by whisking together the first 8 ingredients in a small bowl. Mix until the dressing has blended evenly.

2. Preheat the grill to medium heat. Brush the ears of corn with olive oil and place them directly on the grill, turning occasionally. Grill for about 8 minutes or until the corn is lightly charred.

3. Grill the halved cherry tomatoes for about one minute each, or until light grill marks appear.

4. After everything has cooled, cut the kernels off the cob into a large bowl with the tomatoes. Mix in the spinach and almonds, add the dressing, and toss to achieve an even coating.

 ADD MEAT! Grill up to 1 pound of skinless, boneless chicken breast. Cook each side over medium heat for 5–6 minutes, or until properly heated through. Dice and add this to the salad.

 MAKE IT VEGAN! Replace the goat cheese with another vegan substitute, or serve without cheese.

 GO PALEO! Remove cheese from the recipe.

Balsamic Grilled Plum Salad

ACTIVE TIME: 10 MINUTES • TOTAL TIME: 25 MINUTES • SERVES 4

Grilled plums are a classic, but I especially enjoy how they taste once drizzled in this sweet and tangy balsamic glaze.

1 cup balsamic vinegar
2 teaspoons lemon zest
4 medium, firm plums
½ cup crumbled goat cheese
2 cups baby arugula

1. Cut the plums in half and set aside.

2. Make the balsamic glaze by bringing the balsamic vinegar and lemon zest to a boil in a small saucepan. Cook this until the mixture is thickened and has reduced. This should take about 10–12 minutes, but make sure you're watching it so it doesn't overcook.

3. Preheat your grill to medium heat and place the plums on the grill. Cook for 4–6 minutes, flipping them halfway. Once the plums are tender, remove them from heat and let them cool.

4. After your plums have cooled, cut them into bite-sized cubes and serve over baby arugula.

5. Drizzle the glaze and goat cheese over the salad, and enjoy.

 ADD MEAT! Grill 1 pound of skinless, boneless chicken breast over medium heat for 5–6 minutes per side, or until it has reached desired doneness. After your chicken has cooked, drizzle some of the balsamic glaze mixture over it for extra flavor.

 MAKE IT VEGAN! Replace goat cheese with your favorite vegan substitute from the "Substitutions" chapter.

 GO PALEO! Replace goat cheese with a paleo substitute.

Orzo Salad

This is a fairly simple salad that's easily customized. This dish works just as well as a cold appetizer in the summertime.

1. Cook orzo according to package instructions, drain and let stand.

2. Brush the zucchini and onion with oil, adding salt and pepper to taste. Preheat grill to medium heat.

3. Grill the vegetables covered until they become tender and have slight grill marks, making sure to turn the veggies halfway through. This should take 10–12 minutes.

4. Using a small bowl, mix lemon juice and 1 tablespoon of olive oil until it blends evenly. Combine cooked orzo, vegetables, mozzarella, tomatoes, torn basil and your lemon juice dressing in a large serving bowl. Mix well and sprinkle pine nuts over the top.

8 ounces orzo

1 medium zucchini, cut in half lengthwise

1 medium red onion, cut into quarters

4 tablespoons olive oil

Salt and pepper, to taste

2 tablespoons lemon juice

4 ounces mozzarella cheese, cubed

1 cup grape tomatoes, halved

Fresh basil leaves, torn

¼ cup pine nuts, toasted

 ADD MEAT! Grill 1 or 2 boneless chicken breasts over medium heat until tender, about 3 minutes per side. Remove the chicken, carve into cubes, and then add to salad.

 MAKE IT VEGAN! Replace mozzarella cheese with Moxarella from "Substitutions" chapter.

 GO PALEO! Instead of orzo, try Cauliflower Rice using the recipe in the "Substitutions" chapter. Replace mozzarella cheese with Moxarella.

Grilled Apple Salad

ACTIVE TIME: 15 MINUTES • TOTAL TIME: 30 MINUTES • SERVES 4

Marinating the apples is what makes this recipe stand out. They cook up deliciously and really make this salad amazing.

6 tablespoons olive oil

¼ cup orange juice

¼ cup white balsamic vinegar

¼ cup cilantro

2 tablespoons honey

¼ teaspoon salt

1 clove garlic, minced

3 large apples, cut into wedges

2 ounces baby spinach

3 ounces mixed salad greens

¼ cup slivered almonds

5 ounces goat cheese, crumbled

1. In a small bowl, mix the olive oil, orange juice, vinegar, cilantro, honey, salt and minced garlic. Mix well and pour ¼ cup into a large resealable plastic bag.

2. Add the apples to the bag and marinate for at least 10 minutes in the refrigerator. Refrigerate the remaining dressing for later use.

3. After 10 minutes, drain apples but save the dressing for later use.

4. Skewer the apples and preheat your grill to medium heat. Place the skewered apples on the grill and cook for about 6–8 minutes, or until they become golden brown, flip and grill them for another 6-8 minutes. Remove from heat when they become golden and tender.

5. Once the apples have cooled, chop the wedges into bite-sized pieces. In a large serving bowl, mix the salad greens, slivered almonds and apples. Drizzle the remaining dressing, toss to coat and serve.

 ADD MEAT! Brush some of the orange juice mixture onto 1 pound of skinless, boneless chicken breast and grill for 5–6 minutes per side, or until properly cooked through.

 MAKE IT VEGAN! Replace honey with agave nectar or coconut nectar. Replace the goat cheese with a vegan substitute from the "Substitutions" chapter.

 GO PALEO! Remove or replace the cheese!

Grilled Fruit and Feta Salad

ACTIVE TIME: 15 MINUTES • TOTAL TIME: 25 MINUTES • SERVES 4

The way fruit tastes grilled makes it the ultimate summer treat, in my opinion. In this salad, tangy feta meshes perfectly with the sweetness of the grilled fruits.

1. Preheat your grill to high heat. Grill the watermelon until charred, taking about 2–3 minutes per side.

2. Transfer the grilled watermelon to a cutting board, remove rind, and cube.

3. Brush the onion slices with olive oil and place on the grill. Grill the onion slices until charred, about 5–6 minutes per side. When the slices are tender, remove them from the heat and dice.

4. In a large bowl, toss arugula, watermelon, onion, and feta.

5. In a small bowl, mix together olive oil, balsamic vinegar, red wine vinegar and a pinch of salt. Drizzle this mixture over the salad and toss with a pinch of pepper.

6. Garnish with torn mint leaves and serve.

1 small watermelon, cut into 1-inch-thick rounds

1 small, sweet onion, cut into ½-inch-thick rings

½ cup mint leaves, torn

1 cup baby arugula

2 ounces feta cheese, crumbled

1 tablespoon olive oil

1 tablespoon balsamic vinegar

1 tablespoon red wine vinegar

Salt and pepper, to taste

 ADD MEAT!   Add bits of cooked bacon over the top of the salad.

 MAKE IT VEGAN!   Replace the feta cheese with Moxarella from "Substitutions!"

 GO PALEO!   Replace the feta with any of the paleo substitutes in the "Substitutions" chapter.

Small Plates

There's something especially elegant about making snack food that celebrates refreshing garden goods, rather than mask them in carbs and oil. And these simple dishes can double as full meals for those who don't have hours to spend in the kitchen. Regardless of when you try them, these recipes are surefire hits anywhere from a fancy dinner to a casual barbecue.

Grilled Peapods

Think edamame on the grill. This healthy snack is made for munching on (and fighting over) while you wait for dinner. It's also vegan, paleo and gluten-free so it'll keep everyone happy.

Olive oil and salt, to taste
½ pound of fresh English peapods

1. Prepare your grill for high heat and toss the peapods in olive oil and salt.

2. Place the peapods on the grill and let them cook until they are lightly charred and soft on the inside. This should take a few minutes per side.

3. Move peapods to a serving bowl and enjoy.

 ADD MEAT! Wrap these with half slices of uncooked bacon. Use toothpicks to secure the bacon and grill until the pieces are crisp!

Cajun Green Beans

ACTIVE TIME: 2 MINUTES • **TOTAL TIME: 20 MINUTES** • **SERVES 4**

Requiring almost no effort, this recipe utilizes the natural flavors of the green bean to play off of the notes of Cajun seasoning. You'll barely need your spice cabinet.

1. Prepare a large piece of foil to create a foil packet. Place the green beans on the foil and sprinkle the seasoning over them, dotting with butter. Fold the edges around the beans and crimp the edges to seal the packet tightly.

2. Preheat your grill to medium heat and place the packet on the grill seam side up. Cook for about 20 minutes, rotating the packet about 10 minutes in. Remove from heat when beans are tender and serve.

1 pound green beans, trimmed
½ teaspoon Cajun seasoning
1 tablespoon butter

 ADD MEAT! Remove the packets after about 15 minutes and wrap the green beans in half slices of bacon. Place them back in the foil packets or directly on the grill and cook until the beans are tender and the bacon is crisp.

 MAKE IT VEGAN! Replace the butter with 2¼ teaspoons of olive oil.

Mixed-Vegetable Bruschetta

ACTIVE TIME: 10 MINUTES • TOTAL TIME: 25 MINUTES • SERVES 6

Bruschetta is a wonderful appetizer that can be adjusted in anyway you like. I love making this in the summertime when the zucchini is garden-fresh and plentiful.

1 small zucchini, cut into ¾-inch slices

1 small summer squash, cut into ¾-inch slices

1 rib of celery, cut into ¾-inch slices

2 bell peppers, cut into wedges

1 medium red onion, cut into wedges

I medium tomato, cut into wedges

5 cloves garlic, minced

½ cup olive oil

15 ¼-inch thick slices of French bread

6 fresh basil leaves, torn

1 teaspoon oregano, minced

1 teaspoon parsley, minced

1. In a large bowl, add zucchini, summer squash, celery, peppers, onion and tomato. Add ¼ cup of olive oil and the minced garlic and toss to coat evenly.

2. Preheat grill to medium heat and place the oiled vegetables directly on the grill rack. Grill for 8–10 minutes, turning the vegetables occasionally. When vegetables are tender, remove from heat and let cool. Chop into bite-sized pieces, mix together and set aside in a large bowl.

3. Brush the bread slices on both sides with olive oil. Grill each piece for about 1 minute per side, or until the bread is lightly toasted.

4. Spoon the grilled veggies onto the toast and sprinkle basil leaves, oregano and parsley over the top. Serve and enjoy.

 ADD MEAT! Sprinkle bits of cooked bacon over the bruschetta.

 GO PALEO! Instead of bread, you can use grilled zucchini as your base by cutting it slightly thicker.

 GLUTEN-FREE! See "Go Paleo" variation.

Zucchini Bruschetta

ACTIVE TIME: 10 MINUTES • TOTAL TIME: 15 MINUTES • SERVES 4

These bite-sized bits are sure to make everyone happy, if a little competitive. Feel free to swap out the zucchini for any other squash that you prefer!

3 medium tomatoes, diced

1 large zucchini

2 cloves garlic, minced

¼ cup basil leaves, thinly sliced

1 tablespoon olive oil

1 teaspoon balsamic vinegar

Pinch of salt and pepper

¼ cup mozzarella cheese

1. Preheat grill to medium-high heat. After dicing tomatoes, mix together with basil, olive oil, balsamic vinegar and a pinch of salt and pepper. Set this aside.

2. Slice zucchini into ¼-inch-thick slices and lightly brush them with oil.

3. Grill the zucchini slices for two minutes on each side. Spoon the tomato mixture atop the zucchini and sprinkle mozzarella. Cook for 2 more minutes on the grill, remove from heat and serve.

 ADD MEAT! Cook up a few strips of bacon and crumble them over the top of the zucchini and mozzarella.

 MAKE IT VEGAN! Use the Moxarella recipe from "Substitutions!"

 GO PALEO! Simply remove the cheese from this recipe.

Handheld Guacamole Pockets

ACTIVE TIME: 5 MINUTES • TOTAL TIME: 10 MINUTES • SERVES 4

Avocados are even better when you're able to eat them directly out of their shells. This recipe is a perfect way to keep guests from fighting over the guacamole and requires little-to-no cleanup.

1. Preheat your grill to medium heat. Cut each avocado in half, remove its pit and place on the grill flesh side down.

2. Let the avocados cook until grill marks appear, usually around 3 to 4 minutes. Be sure to monitor the halves to prevent overcooking. Remove your avocados from the grill and squeeze on lime juice, topping with salt, cumin and cilantro. Add diced tomatoes and serve.

4 large avocados, ripe
Pinch of salt
2 limes
¼ cup cilantro, chopped
Pinch of cumin
2 medium tomatoes, diced

 ADD MEAT! Cook up bacon and let it cool until it can be broken easily. Crumble bacon bits over the top for some deliciously meaty avocado.

Vegetable Fried Rice

Who says you can't make fried rice on the grill? This recipe will make you feel like a hibachi chef right in your home. Fried rice is always a crowd favorite, and can easily be made from leftovers, or any vegetables you happen to have sitting around the kitchen. This recipe uses brown rice for some extra nutritional value.

1½ cups uncooked brown rice

4 tablespoons vegetable oil

1 cup fresh bean sprouts

½ cup green peas

½ cup chopped onion

¼ cup chopped scallions

2 eggs (beaten)

4 tablespoons of soy sauce

¼ teaspoon sesame oil

Salt and ground pepper

1. Bring water to a boil in a saucepan. Check your bag of rice for specific cook times and water measurements. Add rice to water and stir. Reduce heat to simmer, and set the timer as directed on the bag of rice. Once the timer goes off, gently move the rice around to ensure that all water has been absorbed.

2. Heat a large cast-iron pan on the grill. Once it's hot, pour in vegetable oil, bean sprouts, green peas, and onions. Mix well and cook for 3 minutes. Mix in rice (it should have cooled by now) and cook for another 3 minutes. Stir constantly.

3. Mix in scallions, eggs, salt, pepper, soy sauce and sesame oil. Cook for approximately 4 more minutes and stir continuously. Make sure eggs are completely cooked and everything has mixed together evenly.

4. Remove rice from the pan and serve.

ADD MEAT! Add 1 pound of skinless, boneless chicken. Trim off all fat and dice chicken before adding. Cook for about 5 to 6 minutes, or until meat begins to brown, and make sure juices run clear before removing from heat.

 MAKE IT VEGAN! Remove eggs from the recipe and trying adding as many different vegetables as you'd like. Try bell peppers, broccoli or zucchini. Broccoli and zucchini take a bit longer to cook, so keep them in the skillet for a tad longer. The great thing about stir fry is that you can always add more veggies.

 GO PALEO! Instead of brown rice, try cauliflower rice, found in the "Substitutions" chapter. Additionally, use coconut aminos instead of soy sauce.

 GLUTEN-FREE! Substitute brown rice with white rice. White rice takes less time to cook than brown rice, so this is a time-saver as well. And be sure to use gluten-free soy sauce, which can be found in most supermarkets.

Grilled Mushroom Skewers

ACTIVE TIME: 5 MINUTES • TOTAL TIME: 20 MINUTES • SERVES 4

Mushroom kebabs are great because they soak up the marinade extremely well. The bell peppers ensure that this skewer is equal parts savory and refreshing.

½ pound medium white mushrooms

2 bell peppers, cut into ½-inch chunks

1 medium onion, cut into ½-inch chunks

¼ cup melted butter

½ teaspoon dill weed

½ teaspoon garlic salt

1. Thread mushrooms, peppers and onions onto 4 skewers.

2. In a small bowl, combine butter, dill and garlic salt. Brush this mixture over the skewers.

3. Preheat grill to medium-high heat and grill skewers for 10–15 minutes, turning occasionally. Remove from heat and serve.

 ADD MEAT! Add steak to the skewers by slicing 1 pound of flank steak into bite-sized cubes. Marinate in the mixture for at least an hour in the refrigerator. Add the cubes to the skewers and grill until they reach desired doneness.

 MAKE IT VEGAN! Replace the butter with olive oil and brush the mixture in the same way.

Balsamic Veggie Skewers

ACTIVE TIME: 30 MINUTES • TOTAL TIME: 30 MINUTES • SERVES 4

Balsamic vinaigrette adds the perfect hint of flavor while allowing the veggies to still express themselves. As we've seen before, skewers keep everyone happy.

1. Begin by cutting your veggies into ³/₄-inch cubes. Try to keep each cube about the same size for all of the vegetables to ensure that they'll all cook for around the same time. Place your vegetable cubes in a large bowl.

2. Make the vinaigrette by whisking all vinaigrette ingredients together in a small bowl. Add vinaigrette to vegetables and toss to coat evenly. Once vegetables are sufficiently coated, begin adding them to skewers in whichever order you prefer.

3. Preheat your grill to medium-high heat. Place skewers directly onto the grates and cook for about 7 minutes, turning occasionally. Remove from heat once lightly charred and grilled to desired tenderness. As a rule of thumb, the edges should be just starting to soften. Serve and enjoy.

VINAIGRETTE:

¼ cup balsamic vinegar

¼ cup olive oil

2 teaspoons Dijon mustard

1 tablespoon lemon juice

2 cloves garlic, minced

Salt and pepper, to taste

VEGGIES:

1 full zucchini

8 small radishes, trimmed

1 large yellow squash

1 small red onion

1 pint grape tomatoes

2 medium-sized bell peppers
(red, yellow or orange)

 ADD MEAT! Double the vinaigrette recipe and use half to marinate steak cubes in a separate bowl. Cut ³/₄ pound of sirloin steak into relatively small cubes—about 1 inch. Toss these in the vinaigrette until they are properly coated. Add the steak cubes onto the skewers before grilling, which should still take about 8 minutes. Be sure to check for desired tenderness while grilling.

 GO VEGAN! This recipe is very vegan-friendly already. Some Dijon mustard may not be vegan, so be sure to check the ingredients.

 GO PALEO! This recipe alone is already paleo, but if you'd like some extra protein I suggest you take a look at the sirloin cubes I mentioned in the "Add Meat" section.

Grilled Avocado Taco Skewers

ACTIVE TIME: 15 MINUTES • TOTAL TIME: 25 MINUTES • SERVES 4

The best part of this recipe is the marinade. Oh, and the fact that you're turning a taco into a kebab.

½ jalapeno, chopped

1½ teaspoons cumin, ground

1 clove garlic, minced

½ cup cilantro, chopped

2 tablespoons lime juice

2 tablespoon vegetable oil

Pinch of salt, to taste

1 avocado, chunked

2 ears corn, shucked and
cut into 1-inch-thick pieces

1 red bell pepper,
cut into 1-inch pieces

1 yellow bell pepper,
cut into 1-inch pieces

2 flour tortillas, cut into triangles

1. Start by making your marinade. In a large bowl, whisk together jalapeno, cumin, garlic, cilantro, lime juice, vegetable oil and salt. Preheat your grill to high.

2. Add the red and yellow bell peppers, avocado, corn and flour tortillas to the large bowl. Toss these with the marinade until they are evenly coated.

3. Skewer the bowl's contents in any order and place on grill. Grill for about 8 minutes, or until kebabs reach desired tenderness. Remove from heat and serve.

 ADD MEAT! Double your marinade ingredients and use half of the marinade for the steak. Start by cutting ¾ pounds of sirloin steak into relatively small cubes—about 1 inch. Toss these in the marinade until they are properly coated. Add these onto the skewers before grilling, which should still take about 8 minutes. Be sure to check for desired tenderness while grilling.

 MAKE IT VEGAN! This recipe is already vegan, but double check that the tortillas you're using don't contain lard.

 GLUTEN-FREE! Use the Paleo Tortillas from "Substitutions."

Butternut Squash Kebabs

ACTIVE TIME: 10 MINUTES • TOTAL TIME: 30 MINUTES • SERVES 6

Butternut squash has a delicious, sweet flavor and lovely texture that is only enhanced by receiving direct heat. As easy to make as it is to adjust, this is a recipe you'll want to keep making.

1 half butternut squash, cut into 1-inch cubes

3 tablespoon butter, melted

1 teaspoon curry powder

Pinch of salt

1. Lightly oil a medium-sized baking dish and place your squash cubes inside.

2. In a small bowl, mix together butter, curry powder and a pinch of salt. Drizzle this mixture over the squash and toss to coat.

3. Bake at 450 degrees F for 20 minutes, stirring occasionally. Remove from heat when tender to cool for a few minutes.

4. Preheat your grill to medium heat and prepare squash by threading the cubes onto skewers. Grill the skewers covered for 7–10 minutes, flipping once halfway through. Remove from heat and serve.

 ADD MEAT! Add steak to the skewers by slicing 1 pound of flank steak into bite-sized cubes. Marinate in the curry mixture for at least an hour in the refrigerator. Add the cubes to the skewers and grill until they reach desired doneness.

 MAKE IT VEGAN! Replace the butter with olive oil and brush the mixture in the same way.

 GO PALEO! This recipe is already, but feel free to add grass-fed flank steak to the skewers.

Pineapple Kebabs

ACTIVE TIME: 20 MINUTES • TOTAL TIME: 30 MINUTES • SERVES 6

These pineapple kebabs grilled with a thick honey glaze make for a perfect blend of sweetness.

1. In a small bowl, mix together pineapple juice, honey, soy sauce, vinegar, garlic and ginger.

2. Pour half of the mixture into a large, resealable bag and add the pineapple chunks and vegetable pieces. Let this marinate for 15 minutes in the refrigerator and then drain and discard the marinade.

3. Thread the pineapple and vegetables onto skewers and arrange them how you prefer.

4. Preheat your grill to medium-high heat and oil the grill grates. Grill the skewers for 8–10 minutes, or until the vegetables are tender. Baste with the remaining marinade while cooking, making sure to turn the skewers occasionally. Remove from heat and serve.

1 (6-ounce) can pineapple juice

⅓ cup honey

⅓ cup soy sauce

3 tablespoons cider vinegar

1 clove garlic, minced

1 teaspoon ginger, ground

1 fresh pineapple,
cut into 1-inch chunks

2 bell peppers,
cut into 1-inch pieces

1 medium zucchini,
cut into 1-inch pieces

1 medium red onion,
cut into 1-inch pieces

 ADD MEAT!   Add 1½ pounds of beef top sirloin steak. Cut the steak into 1-inch pieces. Take ¾ cup of the marinade and place it in a separate resealable bag. Marinate the steak for at least 1 hour in the refrigerator. Add the marinated cubes to the skewers and grill until steak reaches desired doneness.

 MAKE IT VEGAN!   Replace honey with agave nectar or coconut nectar.

 GO PALEO!   Use coconut aminos instead of soy sauce.

 GLUTEN-FREE!   Instead of soy sauce, use coconut aminos or tamari to make this sauce gluten-free.

Teriyaki Zucchini Kebabs

ACTIVE TIME: 20 MINUTES • TOTAL TIME: 50 MINUTES • SERVES 5

No vegetable cookbook would be complete without a teriyaki kebab, and the zucchini absorbs the marinade as well as any vegetable.

1 medium zucchini, cut into 1-inch chunks

3 bell peppers, cut into 1-inch chunks

1 white onion, cut into 1-inch chunks

2 cups cherry tomatoes

1 cup Teriyaki Marinade ("Marinades & Sauces")

Salt, pepper and garlic powder to taste

1. Prepare your grill for medium-high heat. Slice your zucchini, peppers, and onions, and then place them into separate bowls for ease. Mix in your cherry tomatoes.

2. Assemble your kebabs however you prefer until each skewer is full.

3. Sear on grill and reduce heat slightly. Grill for about 10 minutes on each side. Brush on Teriyaki Marinade and cook for about 5 more minutes. Remove and serve.

 ADD MEAT! Try using 2 pounds of boneless, skinless chicken breasts. Slice your chicken into cubes and add them to the desired skewers. Grill for about 10 minutes per side and make sure juices run clear before serving.

 MAKE IT VEGAN! Add cubed tofu to your skewers for some extra protein. These can be grilled for the same amount of time as the rest of the veggies—about 10 minutes per side. Use 28 ounces of tofu for 5 kebabs.

 GO PALEO! Substitute coconut aminos for the marinade. It is possible to make your own glaze, or you can buy a pre-made coconut amino teriyaki glaze.

 GLUTEN-FREE! Substitute marinade with gluten-free soy sauce. Marinate the kebabs in the soy sauce for at least two hours for a richer flavor.

Avocado and Goat Cheese Toast

ACTIVE TIME: 5 MINUTES • TOTAL TIME: 10 MINUTES • SERVES 4

This can easily be a quick breakfast or an afternoon snack. Goat cheese and avocado work perfectly together, making this quick recipe a favorite of mine.

1. Preheat your grill to medium heat. Cut each avocado in half, remove its pit and place on the grill flesh side down.

2. Let avocados cook until grill marks appear, about 3 to 4 minutes. Be sure to monitor the halves to prevent overcooking.

3. Remove from heat and scoop the flesh out into a small bowl. Add in lemon juice, salt and pepper. Mix these ingredients together, but keep the texture slightly chunky.

4. Toast the bread in a toaster or set each piece on the grill for a few minutes.

5. Once the bread is toasted, spread the avocado mixture evenly between the four slices. Top this with arugula, tomato slices, goat cheese and fresh basil. Drizzle with balsamic glaze and serve.

2 avocados
3 tomatoes, sliced
2 teaspoon lemon juice
Pinch of salt and pepper, to taste
4 slices of bread
1 cup arugula, cleaned
2 ounces goat cheese
¼ cup basil leaves, chopped
Balsamic glaze

 ADD MEAT! Sprinkle bits of cooked bacon over the toast to make this even tastier!

 MAKE IT VEGAN! Replace the goat cheese with Moxarella from "Substitutions."

 GO PALEO! Make this paleo by replacing the goat cheese with Macadamia Ricotta Cheese in "Substitutions." Use paleo bread instead of regular bread.

 GLUTEN-FREE! Use gluten-free bread instead of regular bread.

Grilled Avocado Bowls

ACTIVE TIME: 5 MINUTES • TOTAL TIME: 10 MINUTES • SERVES 6

Because we put them on everything, avocados are rare commodities in my house so it's a serious battle whenever they're around. That's why I love this recipe: Each avocado half is the perfect amount for one person and there's no fight over who gets to scrape the bowl clean.

3 avocados

1½ teaspoon lime juice

1½ teaspoon olive oil

Corn Salsa (see "Sides & Salads") or other salsa of your choosing

Dollop of sour cream or vegan Greek-style yogurt

1. Slice avocados in half and remove their pits.

2. In a small bowl, stir lime juice and olive oil together. Brush this on the flesh of the sliced avocados.

3. Preheat grill to medium heat, place avocados flesh side down and cook for 5 minutes, covered. Once slight grill marks appear, remove from heat and add a spoonful of the salsa to the center of the avocados. Top with sour cream.

 ADD MEAT! Cook up a few slices of bacon and crumble them over the salsa.

 MAKE IT VEGAN! Instead of sour cream, serve it with vegan Greek-style yogurt.

 GO PALEO! Remove the sour cream completely and serve as is.

 GLUTEN-FREE! This can still be served with sour cream, as long as you ensure that the sour cream is gluten-free. Most full fat sour creams are gluten-free, but double check before you buy.

Zucchini Rolls

ACTIVE TIME: 20 MINUTES • TOTAL TIME: 30 MINUTES • SERVES 4

The creamy, piquant goat cheese filling makes this a dangerously addictive recipe.

1. Begin by slicing your zucchini lengthwise into ¼-inch slices. Preheat your grill to medium heat.

2. Brush oil onto both sides of your zucchini slices and season with a bit of salt and pepper.

3. Grill for about 8 minutes, flipping once in between. Check for desired tenderness.

4. In a medium bowl, mix together goat cheese, parsley and lemon juice. Ensure that this is mixed thoroughly. This mixture is your filling.

5. Evenly distribute the filling to the grilled zucchini slices, placing the filling about ¼ inch from the end of the slice. Add spinach leaves and as much or as little basil as you'd like and then roll the slices.

6. Place them seam side down on the grill for about 1 minute, using toothpicks to keep rolls intact. Remove from heat and serve.

3 small zucchini

2 tablespoons olive oil

Pinch of salt and pepper, to taste

1½ ounce goat cheese

1 tablespoon parsley, chopped

½ teaspoon lemon juice

2 ounces baby spinach

1 teaspoon basil, chopped

 ADD MEAT! Add bits of cooked, crumbled bacon when making the goat cheese mixture!

 MAKE IT VEGAN! Use the paleo riccota recipe in the "Substitutions" chapter, as this is also vegan.

 GO PALEO! Make this paleo by replacing the goat cheese with Macadamia Ricotta Cheese recipe in "Substitutions."

Grilled Bell Pepper Medley

ACTIVE TIME: 10 MINUTES • TOTAL TIME: 30 MINUTES • SERVES 6

If possible, try using three different bell peppers to make this colorful recipe even more vibrant.

1 pound fresh asparagus, trimmed

3 bell peppers, colors of your choosing

1 medium tomato

1 medium white onion

2 cloves garlic, minced

2 tablespoons olive oil

1 teaspoon parsley, minced

Salt and pepper, to taste

1 teaspoon lemon juice

¼ teaspoon dill weed

1. Create a foil packet by cutting a piece of tinfoil large enough to hold all of the vegetables.

2. Slice vegetables into thin strips.

3. Toss all vegetables with parsley, salt, pepper, lemon, dill weed and olive oil and place on the foil. Fold the foil over, crimp edges and seal to form a packet. Preheat grill to medium heat.

4. Grill packet for 20–25 minutes, or until vegetables are crisp and tender. Open the packet and turn vegetables occasionally. Once the vegetables are tender, remove from heat and serve.

 ADD MEAT! Grill 1 pound of steak with this medley to add additional protein. Prepare the steak for grilling by brushing with olive oil and sprinkling with salt and pepper. Grill each side for about 6 minutes (rare), or until desired tenderness. Slice and serve.

Balsamic Eggplant and Squash

ACTIVE TIME: 10 MINUTES • TOTAL TIME: 15 MINUTES • SERVES 4

Balsamic anything brings me a lot of joy. This dish goes great when served over pasta or rice and can be easily customized to fit all diets.

1 medium summer squash

1 small eggplant

⅓ cup feta cheese, crumbled

Balsamic Marinade ("Marinades & Sauces")

1. Begin by creating your marinade using the Balsamic Marinade recipe in the "Marinades & Sauces" section.

2. Cut your squash and eggplant into ¼-inch-thick slices and brush with the balsamic.

3. Place the pieces on the grill and cook for 10–12 minutes, turning the pieces occasionally.

4. Remove from heat when they turn golden brown. Top with the feta and serve.

 ADD MEAT! Serve this dish with 1 pound of flank steak. Prepare the steak for grilling by marinating with the Balsamic Marinade for at least 1 hour in the refrigerator. Grill each side for about 6 minutes (rare), or until desired tenderness. Slice and serve with the squash.

 MAKE IT VEGAN! Replace the feta cheese with the Moxarella recipe from "Substitutions."

Grilled Zucchini Nachos

Serve zucchini nacho style for a fun twist on a classic dish. This is sure to please everyone at the table.

1. Prepare your nachos by slicing zucchini into ¼-inch-thick slices, like chips.

2. Rinse and drain the black beans, dice the tomatoes, slice avocado in half, remove seeds and chop. Chop cilantro and onions as well.

3. Place sliced zucchini in a medium bowl and toss with olive oil, seasoning with salt and pepper.

4. Preheat grill to medium heat and place zucchini chips on grill. Cook the chips until the zucchini is tender, about 4–5 minutes. Sprinkle cheese over the zucchini chips and continue cooking until the cheese is slightly melted. This should take about 1 minute.

5. Place cooked chips on a large platter, top with black beans, tomatoes, avocado, onion, cilantro and a squeeze of lime juice. Serve and enjoy.

2 medium zucchini

1 cup shredded cheddar cheese

1 (15-ounce) can black beans

1 large tomato

1 large avocado

2 green onions

¼ cup cilantro

1 lime

Salt and pepper, to taste

¼ cup olive oil

 ADD MEAT! Grill 1 pound of skinless, boneless chicken over medium heat for 5–6 minutes per side. Remove from heat and dice the chicken. Toss the chicken over the nachos and enjoy.

 MAKE IT VEGAN! Simply remove the cheddar cheese from the recipe. You can find vegan cheese at most supermarkets, or you can use the Moxarella recipe from "Substitutions."

 GO PALEO! Remove the cheese and black beans from the recipe. It will still be great without them, promise.

Stuffed Portobello Caps

ACTIVE TIME: 25 MINUTES • TOTAL TIME: 25 MINUTES • SERVES 4

These make the perfect individual meal. You can easily save these caps for another meal or share them. They're incredibly easy to make and taste wonderful.

4 large portobello mushrooms

3 teaspoons olive oil

½ cup grape tomatoes, diced

1 clove garlic, minced

2 tablespoons fresh mozzarella

1 green onion, thinly sliced

1 small white onion, diced

1 red bell pepper, diced

1 loaf sourdough, toasted and chopped into fine breadcrumbs

1. Preheat grill to medium heat. Remove stems and gills from mushrooms.

2. Brush the mushrooms with oil and grill for 2 minutes on each side, or until they begin to soften. Remove from heat and use paper towels to remove excess moisture from the insides of the caps.

3. Fill the caps with tomatoes, garlic, mozzarella and both onions. Grill for another 6–8 minutes, stuffing side up.

4. Remove from heat and top with sourdough breadcrumbs. Serve immediately.

 ADD MEAT! These go great with your favorite cut of steak. Grill 1 pound of your favorite type of steak and prepare the steak for grilling by brushing with olive oil and sprinkling with salt and pepper. Grill each side for about 6 minutes (rare) over medium heat, or until desired tenderness. Dice and add this to the salad.

 MAKE IT VEGAN! Replace mozzarella cheese with Moxarella from "Substitutions."

 GO PALEO! Replace the mozzarella with "Macadamia Ricotta Cheese" from "Substitutions."

Stuffed Pesto Peppers

ACTIVE TIME: 10 MINUTES • TOTAL TIME: 35 MINUTES • SERVES 4

Pesto is delicious, peppers are delicious—why not combine them and make something magical?

1. Brush corn lightly with oil.

2. Preheat grill to medium-high heat. Place 2 ears of corn directly on the grill. Turn the corn and grill for about 8 minutes, or until corn becomes lightly charred and kernels have browned. Let these cool for a bit, and cut the kernels from the cob into a bowl.

3. Make your pesto by combining ½ cup of olive oil, Parmesan cheese, basil, sunflower kernels, and garlic in a food processor. Cover and process until blended completely.

4. Heat olive oil in a large skillet over medium heat. Cook the chopped red pepper until tender, add the corn and pesto and heat through.

5. While this is cooking, cut the bell peppers in half lengthwise and remove their seeds.

6. Grill the pepper halves over medium heat, covered with the cut side facing down. Cook these for about 8 minutes. Flip them over and fill with the pesto mixture. Grill them 4–6 minutes longer, or until they've reached desired tenderness. Serve and enjoy.

Olive oil; ½ cup and 2 teaspoons (keep separate)

¼ cup Parmesan cheese, grated

2 cups basil leaves

2 tablespoons sunflower kernels

4 cloves garlic

½ cup finely chopped sweet red pepper

2 medium ears of corn, shucked

4 medium bell peppers, any color

 ADD MEAT! Crumbled prosciutto bits can be sprinkled over the tops of the peppers.

 MAKE IT VEGAN! Replace the regular Parmesan cheese with the "Paleo Parmesan Cheese" from "Substitutions." Or remove it entirely.

 GO PALEO! Just as in the vegan variation, you'll want to remove or replace the cheese.

Nutty Stuffed Mushrooms

ACTIVE TIME: 15 MINUTES • TOTAL TIME: 35 MINUTES • SERVES 4

These mini mushrooms make a great meal or snack, depending on how many you want to eat. I like to make them using fresh mushrooms and basil leaves!

24 fresh cremini mushrooms

4 green onions, chopped

Fresh basil leaves

2 tablespoons pine nuts

¼ cup Cheddar cheese

¼ cup olive oil

Salt and pepper, to taste

1. Remove stems from mushrooms and preheat grill to high heat.

2. Prepare 2 large sheets of aluminum foil. Make sure foil is large enough for all 24 mushrooms. The second piece of foil will be used to cover the top and to create a packet.

3. Stuff each mushroom with green onion, torn basil and pine nuts. Drizzle the mushrooms with olive oil then sprinkle with Cheddar cheese, salt and pepper. Seal the foil packet.

4. Place on grill and cook for 20 minutes, or until mushrooms become tender. Remove from heat and serve.

 ADD MEAT! Cook a few slices of salami until slightly crisp, tear and crumble over the mushrooms.

 MAKE IT VEGAN! Replace the cheese with the "Paleo Parmesan Cheese" in "Substitutions!"

 GO PALEO! Just as in the vegan variation, replace the cheese.

Stuffed Tomatoes

ACTIVE TIME: 15 MINUTES • TOTAL TIME: 25 MINUTES • SERVES 6

Stuffed tomatoes are nice on their own, but they reach new heights once cooked on a grill. If you want to introduce more flavor, try adding carrots, celery or bell peppers.

6 large tomatoes

2 tablespoons green onions, chopped

1 tablespoon basil leaves, torn

6 ounces goat cheese

2 cups cooked orzo

3 tablespoons olive oil

Salt and pepper, to taste

1. Preheat your grill to medium heat. To prepare the tomatoes, cut off enough of the top to scoop out the insides. Remove all seeds and juice and discard.

2. In a medium bowl, mix together onions, basil, goat cheese and cooked orzo. Season with salt and mix thoroughly.

3. Using this mixture, evenly distribute and stuff the tomatoes. Lightly drizzle with olive oil and place on the grill.

4. With lid closed, cook the stuffed tomatoes for about 10 minutes, or until juices run. Remove from heat and serve.

 ADD MEAT! Add 1 pound of lean ground beef. Cook and stir the beef in a skillet with olive oil until it turns golden brown. Add your beef when making the orzo mixture.

 MAKE IT VEGAN! Replace goat cheese with Moxarella from the "Substitutions" chapter.

 GO PALEO! Instead of orzo, try Cauliflower Rice from the "Substitutions." Replace goat cheese with Macadamia Ricotta Cheese.

Summer Squash Bites

ACTIVE TIME: 10 MINUTES • TOTAL TIME: 25 MINUTES • SERVES 4

These little squash bites are an amazing snack or meal, depending on how many you want to eat. Once again, squash shows its star power amongst grilled vegetables.

1. Preheat your grill to medium-high heat. Cut your squash into 1/4-inch slices.

2. In a small bowl, mix butter and garlic and set aside.

3. Cut a piece of foil large enough to hold every slice. Arrange the squash slices on the foil and brush both sides with the butter mixture. Sprinkle Parmesan cheese, thyme and oregano on top and place the foil on the grill.

4. Cook the slices until they become tender and the cheese melts. This should take about 12–15 minutes. Remove from heat and serve.

2 tablespoon butter
1 clove garlic, minced
1 large summer squash
1 large zucchini
Pinch of thyme and oregano
1/3 cup Parmesan cheese, shredded

 ADD MEAT! Add chicken or replace the squash with it. Coat 1 pound of skinless, boneless chicken in the same way you'd coat the squash and grill for 5–6 minutes per side, or until it is completely cooked through. Top with Parmesan cheese and cook until cheese melts.

 MAKE IT VEGAN! Use Moxarella or Vegan Parmesan Cheese from "Substitutions." Additionally, use olive oil instead of butter.

 GO PALEO! Use the Vegan Parmesan Cheese recipe from "Substitutions."

Feta Zucchini Chips

ACTIVE TIME: 10 MINUTES • TOTAL TIME: 20 MINUTES • SERVES 4

This amazing snack won't be found at most barbecues, but carries a much more interesting flavor profile than your standard potato chip. Try these with a dip of your choosing or just eat them on their own.

2 large zucchini

¼ cup olive oil

1⅓ cups feta cheese, crumbled

1 teaspoon garlic powder

1 teaspoon basil

1 teaspoon oregano

1. Preheat your grill to medium-high heat. Cut your zucchini into ¼-inch slices.

2. Brush the zucchini with olive oil on both sides. Top with feta, garlic powder, basil and oregano. Sprinkle the herbs lightly.

3. Cut a piece of foil large enough to hold all of the slices. Top with zucchini slices and place the foil on the grill.

4. Cook the slices until they become tender and the cheese melts. This should take about 10–12 minutes. Remove from heat and serve.

 ADD MEAT! Crumble cooked bacon bits over the chips and serve.

 MAKE IT VEGAN! Use Moxarella from "Substitutions."

 GO PALEO! Replace the cheese with any paleo cheese from "Substitutions," or remove it completely.

Grilled Acorn Squash

ACTIVE TIME: 15 MINUTES • TOTAL TIME: 1 HOUR • SERVES 6

While this recipe takes a bit longer to make than most, it is truly worth it. This is the perfect autumn meal. When the leaves are falling and the temperature is dropping, warm up with this amazing squash.

3 acorn squash

3 tablespoons molasses

1 teaspoon salt

¼ teaspoon pepper

1 teaspoon ginger

2 tablespoons butter

¼ teaspoon allspice

1. Cut acorn squash in half, lengthwise.

2. Cut pieces of foil large enough to create sealed foil packets. Place the squash flesh side down on its own piece of foil. Wrap foil tightly around the squash half and crimp edges to seal.

3. Preheat grill to medium heat, place the foil packet on the grill and cook until squash becomes tender. This should take about 30 minutes.

4. In a small bowl, mix together the remaining ingredients and let sit.

5. Once the squash has finished cooking, remove from heat and carefully open the foil packets. Spoon the molasses mixture into the squash cavities, reseal the foil and cook for another 30 minutes. Remove from heat when squash is tender and serve.

 ADD MEAT! This recipe goes great with a rack of ribs.

 MAKE IT VEGAN! Use 4 ½ teaspoons of olive oil instead of the butter.

 GO PALEO! Make sure you are using pure molasses.

Grilled Kale Chips

ACTIVE TIME: 10 MINUTES • TOTAL TIME: 15 MINUTES • SERVES 4

This is a quick and easy recipe for those who want a guilt-free snack. Kale chips are becoming hugely popular in most restaurants, and for good reason! They're incredibly easy to make, and you can eat as many as you want and still feel good.

1. Preheat your grill to medium heat. Separate stems from dry kale leaves.

2. In a large mixing bowl, toss the kale, olive oil, balsamic vinegar, garlic and lemon juice. Add a pinch of salt and pepper for seasoning and make sure the kale is evenly coated after mixing.

3. Gently place the kale in a single layer on the grill and cook until it becomes crispy, which should take about 2 minutes. Be sure to grill both sides of the kale until crispy. Take them off of the heat and serve right away.

2 bunches of dry kale leaves
1 cup olive oil
2 cloves of garlic (minced)
1 tablespoon balsamic vinegar
Juice of one lemon
Salt and pepper

 ADD MEAT! Grill up 1 pound of skinless, boneless chicken breast on medium-high heat for 5 to 6 minutes per side, or until meat is cooked through. Remove from heat and dice. Break the kale into larger pieces and toss them in a salad, adding the grilled chicken on top.

 MAKE IT VEGAN! Break into larger pieces and toss them in a salad. Toss with diced bell peppers, cucumbers and shredded carrots!

 GLUTEN-FREE! This recipe is already gluten-free—just be sure to use vinegars that do not contain gluten.

Pesto Mushrooms

ACTIVE TIME: 10 MINUTES • TOTAL TIME: 20 MINUTES • SERVES 4

I love mushrooms in any form, but they taste best when grilled and topped with fresh pesto.

MUSHROOMS

4 large portobello mushrooms

2 tablespoons olive oil

1 clove garlic, minced

Pinch of salt

4 ounces feta cheese

PESTO

½ cup olive oil

¼ cup Parmesan cheese, grated

2 cups basil leaves

2 tablespoons sunflower kernels

4 cloves garlic

1. Begin by making the pesto. Combine ½ cup of olive oil, Parmesan cheese, basil, sunflower kernels and garlic in a food processor. Cover and process until blended completely.

2. Remove the stems from the portobello mushrooms and remove the gills with a spoon.

3. In a small bowl, mix together the minced garlic and 2 tablespoons of olive oil. Brush the mixture over the mushrooms and sprinkle them with salt.

4. In small bowl, combine the pesto and feta cheese and set aside.

5. Preheat grill to medium heat, place the mushrooms stems side up on a piece of foil and place this on the grill. Grill, covered, for 8–10 minutes, or until the mushrooms have become tender.

6. Spoon the feta mixture into the caps and grill for 2–3 more minutes, or until the cheese has just begun to melt. Remove from heat and serve.

 ADD MEAT! Top these portobellos with strips of bacon crumbled over the pesto, or cook a few slices of prosciutto and toss those on top.

 MAKE IT VEGAN! Replace the feta with Moxarella and replace the Parmesan with Vegan Parmesan Cheese from "Substitutions."

 GO PALEO! Remove and replace the cheeses with paleo cheese from the supermarket.

Grilled Radishes

ACTIVE TIME: 5 MINUTES • TOTAL TIME: 25 MINUTES • SERVES 4

Radishes, in their spicy complexity, are a wonderful option if you're looking to wake up your palate before a hearty meal.

1. Preheat your grill to high heat and prepare a large piece of tin foil to make a packet. Place the sliced radishes and ice cube on the foil. Brush with oil and fold to crimp and seal the packet, making sure it is sealed tightly.

2. Place the packet on the grill and cook for 20 minutes, or until the radishes are tender. Remove from heat, add salt and pepper to taste and serve.

20 ounces radishes, sliced

2 cloves garlic, minced

2 tablespoons olive oil

1 cube ice

Salt and pepper, to taste

 ADD MEAT! Serve this with some steak brushed with oil and garlic and sprinkled with a little bit of salt and pepper. Grill each side for about 6 minutes (rare) over medium heat, or until desired tenderness. Slice it up and serve.

Caramelized Romaine Hearts

ACTIVE TIME: 10 MINUTES • TOTAL TIME: 15 MINUTES • SERVES 4

These hunks of sweet lettuce are a nice match with pork chops or quinoa.

1. Preheat your grill to high heat and lightly oil the grate to prevent sticking. Toss the lettuce halves with olive oil.

2. Place the lettuce on the grill cut side down and cook until that side begins to caramelize. This should take about 5 minutes.

3. Remove from heat and place cut side up on a serving plate. Sprinkle cheese and drizzle balsamic vinegar, red wine vinegar and olive oil on top. Serve and enjoy.

3 hearts romaine lettuce, cut in half lengthwise

1 tablespoon olive oil

2 tablespoons Parmesan cheese

2 tablespoons balsamic vinegar

2 tablespoons red wine vinegar

2 tablespoons olive oil

 ADD MEAT! Serve this with pork chops. In a small bowl, combine 2 cloves of minced garlic, 1 cup of fresh, minced basil leaves, 2 tablespoons of lemon juice, 2 tablespoons of olive oil and a pinch of salt and pepper. Spread this over 4 bone-in pork loin chops and marinate for 30-45 minutes. Grill over medium heat for about 6 minutes on each side, or until the pork chops are tender.

 MAKE IT VEGAN! Replace the cheese with one of the vegan cheese options in "Substitutions."

 GO PALEO! Remove the cheese and serve with the pork chops described in the "Add Meat" variation.

 GLUTEN-FREE! Serve over $1/2$ cup cooked quinoa.

Portobello Mozzarella Caps

ACTIVE TIME: 15 MINUTES • TOTAL TIME: 45 MINUTES • SERVES 4

Portobello mushrooms are like their own little, personal dish. After being marinated in Italian dressing, they're the perfect little meal.

4 portobello mushroom caps

1 (8-ounce) bottle Italian dressing

2 bell peppers, sliced

2 tablespoons olive oil

10 ounces fresh mozzarella

½ teaspoon dried oregano

6 basil leaves, torn

1. Fill a large resealable bag with salad dressing, add the mushroom caps and let sit for 15 minutes. Preheat grill to medium-high heat.

2. Brush the sliced bell peppers with olive oil and place on the grill. Place the marinated mushroom caps on the grill as well. Cook mushrooms for 7–10 minutes and bell peppers for 4–5 minutes, or until both become tender. Turn the mushrooms and peppers occasionally, removing from heat when they are lightly charred.

3. Cut the pepper strips into small chunks.

4. Place the mushroom caps bottom side up and place mozzarella on top. Place on the grill until the cheese starts to melt, about 3 minutes.

5. Remove from heat, add the chopped peppers on top and serve.

 ADD MEAT!   Add crumbled bits of cooked bacon into the mushroom caps.

 MAKE IT VEGAN!   Use the vegan Moxarella from "Substitutions."

 GO PALEO!   Remove the cheese from this recipe and replace with any other paleo cheese option.

Zucchini Shells

ACTIVE TIME: 10 MINUTES • TOTAL TIME: 45 MINUTES • SERVES 4

Fill these zucchini shells up with your favorite veggies and enjoy.

4 medium zucchini

1 tablespoon olive oil

1 yellow or white onion, chopped

8 ounces button mushrooms, sliced

2 cloves garlic, minced

1 teaspoon coriander, ground

1 teaspoon cumin

1 (15-ounce) can chickpeas

1 tablespoon lemon juice

2 tablespoons basil, chopped

Salt and pepper, to taste

1. Cut zucchini in half lengthwise and brush with oil. Scoop out the flesh of the zucchini, chop and set aside.

2. Heat oil in a skillet and begin sautéing onions. Sauté for about 5 minutes, add garlic and sauté for 2 more minutes. Mix in the chopped zucchini flesh and mushrooms, and then continue sautéing for 5 more minutes. Mix in the coriander, cumin, chickpeas, lemon juice and basil.

3. Brush oil on the outside of the shells and spoon the mixture into the zucchini shells.

4. Preheat your grill to medium heat and oil the grates. Place the shells on the grill and cook covered for about 20 minutes, or until zucchini is tender. Serve and enjoy.

 ADD MEAT! Cooked bacon sprinkled on these shells is super delicious.

 GO PALEO! Since beans aren't paleo, kick them right out of this recipe.

Bite-sized Zucchini Pizza

ACTIVE TIME: 20 MINUTES • TOTAL TIME: 25 MINUTES • SERVES 4

Enjoy these "pizzas" without the customary guilt, and have fun customizing your toppings as well.

1. Preheat grill to medium heat. Cut your zucchini into rounds of desired thickness.

2. In a small bowl, combine the melted butter and garlic.

3. Lay your zucchini slices on the grill and cook for about 2 minutes. Flip the slices over and brush on the garlic-butter mixture. Cook for about 3 more minutes and then flip over. Repeat process for the newly flipped side.

4. Cover the slices in sauce and mozzarella cheese and cook until the cheese is slightly melted. Remove from heat and serve.

1 large zucchini
½ cup melted butter
2 cloves garlic (minced)
½ cup mozzarella cheese
15 ounces pizza sauce

 ADD MEAT! Add pepperoni slices for a bit of meat.

 MAKE IT VEGAN! Replace the mozzarella with the Moxarella recipe found in "Substitutions."

 GO PALEO! Use the Paleo Pizza Sauce recipe in "Substitutions" to ensure that this recipe is paleo-friendly!

 GLUTEN-FREE! This recipe is already gluten-free, but make sure that the mozzarella cheese you are using does not contain vinegar.

Zucchini Pesto Rolls

ACTIVE TIME: 10 MINUTES • TOTAL TIME: 20 MINUTES • SERVES 4

A combination of my two favorite things that are sure to go fast at any gathering.

1. Make the pesto by combining basil leaves, garlic and walnuts in a food processor. Make sure it's well blended by pouring in the ½ cup of olive oil gradually. Add the Parmesan cheese and pulse again until your pesto evenly blended. Add salt and pepper as desired.

2. Slice the zucchini lengthwise into ¼-inch-thick pieces.

3. Preheat grill to medium heat and brush the slices with olive oil. Grill for about 1 minute per side, or until slight grill marks appear. Once they are tender, remove from heat and let them cool slightly.

4. Distribute the pesto between the slices and spread. Roll up the slices, secure them with a toothpick and serve.

1 cup basil leaves
1 clove garlic
¼ cup walnuts
½ cup olive oil
¼ cup Parmesan cheese, grated
6 medium zucchini
Salt and pepper, to taste

 ADD MEAT! Mix bits of cooked bacon into the pesto.

 MAKE IT VEGAN! Remove the cheese and replace it with one of the substitute options.

 GO PALEO! Use a paleo cheese alternative from your local supermarket.

Quinoa Spinach Mushrooms

ACTIVE TIME: 20 MINUTES • TOTAL TIME: 40 MINUTES • SERVES 6

These are a nice source of protein thanks to the spinach and quinoa. It's also super easy to save this dish for meals throughout the week.

⅓ cup quinoa, uncooked

1 tablespoon olive oil

¼ cup shallots, minced

4 cloves garlic, minced

6 ounces baby spinach

3 ounces feta cheese, crumbled

Salt and pepper, to taste

30 large cremini mushrooms, stems removed

1. Cook quinoa according to package instructions, remove from heat and let stand.

2. Heat a skillet with oil and add shallots and garlic, cooking until they become slightly brown and tender. This process should take about 5 minutes. Toss in spinach and cook, stirring regularly until the spinach wilts.

3. Remove from heat and add to a large bowl, mixing in quinoa, cheese, salt and pepper.

4. Brush mushroom caps with oil, arrange them on a large piece of foil and preheat your grill to medium heat. Fill the caps with the quinoa mixture, distributing evenly.

5. Create a foil packet by placing a large piece of foil on top, crimping and sealing edges. Carefully place the packet on the grill and let the mushrooms cook, covered, for about 20 minutes —or until they become tender. Remove from heat and serve.

 ADD MEAT! Prepare ½ pound of steak for grilling by brushing with olive oil and sprinkling with salt and pepper. Grill each side for about 6 minutes over medium heat, or until it reaches desired tenderness. Dice and serve with your mushrooms.

 MAKE IT VEGAN! Remove or replace the feta in this recipe!

 GO PALEO! Since quinoa is not paleo, serve this with white rice instead, or make Cauliflower Rice from "Substitutions." Additionally, remove the cheese completely, or replace it with one of the vegan alternatives.

Easy Garlic Corn on the Cob

ACTIVE TIME: 5 MINUTES • TOTAL TIME: 15 MINUTES • SERVES 4

Easy, yes—but this dish is far from basic. Garlic, oil and corn—with its natural sweetness—are a combination you'll never tire of. Serve this pre-dinner or alongside whatever else is on the grill.

1. In a small bowl, mix garlic and olive oil together. Brush this mixture over the corn so that each ear is completely coated. Sprinkle sugar over the corn and preheat the grill to medium heat.

2. Place the corn on a large sheet of foil, fold, and crimp the edges to seal the packet tightly. Place the corn packets on the grill and cook for 10–15 minutes, or until the corn becomes tender. Turn the packets occasionally and remove from heat once the corn is tender. Serve and enjoy.

4 cloves garlic, minced
2 tablespoons olive oil
4 ears corn, shucked
1 teaspoon sugar

 ADD MEAT! Serve this with steak! Prepare the steak for grilling by brushing with olive oil and sprinkling with salt and pepper. Grill each side over medium heat for at least 6 minutes. Dice and add to the salad.

 GO PALEO! Completely remove the sugar from this recipe.

Grilled Potatoes

ACTIVE TIME: 15 MINUTES • TOTAL TIME: 55 MINUTES • SERVES 6

Cut your delicious spuds into fans in order to maximize topping space.

6 medium white potatoes

2 medium white onions

6 tablespoons butter, cut in cubes

¼ cup celery, chopped

1 teaspoon salt

1 teaspoon dried oregano

1 clove garlic, minced

Pinch of pepper

1. Rinse and dry your potatoes. Prepare them by making multiple cuts about ½ inch apart in each potato, making sure to leave the slices attached to the skin to create a fan. Slightly fan the potatoes.

2. Cut 6 large pieces of foil to create packets for the potatoes. Between the potato slices, place butter and onions. Sprinkle on celery, salt, oregano, garlic and pepper. Fold the foil around the potatoes so that they're tightly sealed.

3. Preheat your grill to medium-high heat and place the 6 packets on the grill. Grill covered until the potatoes become tender, which should take about 40 minutes. Remove from heat and serve.

 ADD MEAT! Enhance these potatoes by crumbling cooked bacon bits on top.

 MAKE IT VEGAN! Replace the butter with 4½ tablespoons of olive oil.

 GO PALEO! Use sweet potatoes instead!

Stuffed Jalapenos

ACTIVE TIME: 10 MINUTES • TOTAL TIME: 15 MINUTES • SERVES 4

These are a quick and easy snack or a full meal, depending on how many peppers you want. Stuffed jalapenos have a nice kick to them that's tempered perfectly by the cream cheese mixture!

1. In a small bowl, combine cream cheese, pepper jack, garlic powder, cumin and a pinch of salt and paprika. Mix well.

2. Cut slits in each pepper, lengthwise. Hollow them out and fill them with the cream cheese mixture.

3. Preheat grill to medium heat, place the peppers on the grill and cook for 8–10 minutes, or until tender. Once cheese is melted and the peppers are tender, remove from heat and serve.

4 ounce cream cheese, softened
½ cup pepper jack cheese, shredded
½ teaspoon garlic powder
½ teaspoon ground cumin
Salt, to taste
Pinch of paprika
10 jalapeno peppers

 ADD MEAT! Add 1 pound of ground pork sausage. Cook in a small skillet until it becomes golden brown and add it to the cream cheese mixture.

 MAKE IT VEGAN! Replace cream cheese with almond cream cheese that's been prepared the night before. Simply soak 1 cup of raw almonds in ½ cup of water for 8 hours, drain and rinse. Pour very hot water on the almonds and let them sit for 5 minutes to blanch them. Remove the skins from the almonds and place them in a food processor with water, a pinch of salt, 1 teaspoon of apple cider vinegar and 1 teaspoon of lemon juice. Blend until mixture becomes smooth. Additionally, use the Moxarella recipe from the "Substitutions" chapter, rather than pepper jack.

 GO PALEO! The vegan variation on cream cheese is also paleo. Leave the pepper jack out of the recipe.

Garlic Stuffed Tomatoes

ACTIVE TIME: 15 MINUTES • TOTAL TIME: 30 MINUTES • SERVES 6

These stuffed tomatoes are a simple yet elegant dish. They're perfect if you're entertaining company or even just to save for later.

6 medium tomatoes

1 cup garlic croutons, crushed

2 tablespoon Parmesan cheese, grated

2 tablespoon cheddar cheese, grated

4 tablespoon butter, melted

Salt and pepper, to taste

Fresh basil leaves, torn

1. Cut a ¼-inch-thick slice off of the top of the tomato and scoop out the pulp in order to leave a shell. Try to drain the tomatoes as best you can over paper towels.

2. While the tomatoes are draining, mix together the remaining ingredients in a medium bowl. Once the mixture is thoroughly mixed, evenly distribute between the four tomato shells. Sprinkle the torn basil over the top.

3. Preheat grill to medium heat and brush the grates with olive oil. Place the tomatoes on the oiled grates and grill covered for about 10 minutes. Remove from heat once the mixture has heated through and serve.

 ADD MEAT! Add 1 pound of lean ground beef. Cook and stir the beef in a skillet with olive oil until it turns golden brown and add to the rest of the stuffing.

 MAKE IT VEGAN! Find cheese alternatives in "Substitutions." Replace the butter with 3 tablespoons of olive oil.

 GO PALEO! Remove croutons from the recipe and replace the cheeses with paleo substitutes from the supermarket.

 GLUTEN-FREE! Remove the croutons from the recipe. Gluten-free croutons can be found at most supermarkets if you want to keep them as part of the recipe.

Mushroom Napoleon

ACTIVE TIME: 10 MINUTES • TOTAL TIME: 40 MINUTES • SERVES 4

This isn't your classic napoleon pastry. This is a deliciously layered mushroom napoleon. It may not be as sweet as a regular napoleon, but I like savory better anyway.

4 large portobello mushrooms

1 bell pepper, sliced

1 small red onion, cut into 8 wedges

¼ cup red wine vinegar

1 tablespoon Dijon mustard

1 teaspoon sugar

Salt and pepper, to taste

½ cup olive oil

4 small tomatoes, cut into slices

Fresh basil leaves, torn

1 cup goat cheese, crumbled

1. In a large resealable bag, mix red wine vinegar, Dijon mustard, sugar, olive oil and a pinch of salt and pepper. Add the mushrooms, bell pepper slices and onion into the bag. Toss to coat and let marinate for about 30 minutes in the refrigerator. Drain and save the marinade for later use.

2. Preheat your grill to medium-high heat and coat the grates with oil. Place the mushrooms, bell pepper and onion on the grill and cook for 7–8 minutes per side, or until the vegetables become tender.

3. Remove from heat and serve by placing the mushrooms gill side up. Stack with peppers, onions, tomato slices and basil. Sprinkle with cheese and drizzle remaining marinade over the stacks. Serve and enjoy.

 ADD MEAT! Add small pieces of cooked bacon to each stack. Slice the bacon into small bits if necessary.

 MAKE IT VEGAN! Replace the goat cheese with one from the "Substitutions" section.

 GO PALEO! Replace or remove the goat cheese.

Cheesy Grilled Tomatoes

ACTIVE TIME: 15 MINUTES • TOTAL TIME: 25 MINUTES • SERVES 6

Like a tomato grill cheese, only with fewer carbs.

1. Sprinkle the cut side of the tomatoes with cheese, breadcrumbs, onions and butter, distributing evenly between the tomatoes. Add a pinch of salt to each and preheat your grill to medium heat.

2. Place the tomatoes cut side up on the grill and cook for 6–8 minutes or until the cheese melts and tomatoes are tender. Remove from heat and serve.

6 plum tomatoes, halved lengthwise
½ cup blue cheese, crumbled
¼ cup dry bread crumbs
¼ cup red onion, grated
2 tablespoons butter, melted
Pinch of salt

 ADD MEAT! Bacon bits make this a savory snack, but grill 1 pound of boneless, skinless chicken breast for 6 minutes on each side if you want a more filling meal.

 MAKE IT VEGAN! Replace cheese with Macadamia Ricotta Cheese from the "Substitutions" section and butter with 1½ tablespoons of olive oil.

 GO PALEO! Replace cheese with Macadamia Ricotta Cheese. For a bread-crumb replacement, combine 1 cup of almond flour or almond meal, ½ teaspoon of salt, ½ teaspoon of black pepper, ½ teaspoon of garlic powder, ½ teaspoon of dried parsley, ¼ teaspoon of onion powder and ¼ teaspoon of dried oregano in a small bowl.

 GLUTEN-FREE! Replace the breadcrumbs with the paleo variation detailed above.

Salsa-Stuffed Peppers

ACTIVE TIME: 10 MINUTES • TOTAL TIME: 25 MINUTES • SERVES 4

Bell peppers are the perfect vessel for a great stuffing. These peppers are really easy to make and don't take much time. One pepper per person is plenty!

1. In a medium bowl, combine the corn, tomatoes, onions and chili peppers and drain slightly. Stir in the vinegar and salt.

2. Distribute the mixture between the pepper halves and place each pepper on a large piece of foil. Fold the foil around the peppers and crimp the edges, forming a tightly sealed packet.

3. Preheat grill to medium heat and place the packets on the grill. Cook until the peppers are tender, which should take about 20–25 minutes.

4. Remove the packets from the grill and sprinkle cheese over the peppers. Return these to grill until the cheese has melted (about 3–5 minutes), remove from heat and serve.

4 large tomatoes, chopped

2 cups frozen corn, thawed

1 white onion, chopped

¾ cup green chili peppers, chopped

1 teaspoon vinegar

1 teaspoon salt

2 bell peppers, halved and seeds removed

½ cup pepper jack cheese, shredded

 ADD MEAT! Add two strips of cooked bacon. Sprinkle crumbled bacon when sprinkling on cheese, and return to the grill.

 MAKE IT VEGAN! Replace the cheese with the Moxarella from the "Substitutions" section.

 GO PALEO! Remove the cheese from this recipe.

Grilled Orange Mushrooms

ACTIVE TIME: 15 MINUTES • TOTAL TIME: 25 MINUTES • SERVES 6

The orange juice and zest really give these mushrooms a unique flavor.
This recipe is super easy to make and tastes great.

1 cup orange juice

¼ cup olive oil

4 teaspoon orange zest

Salt and pepper, to taste

½ pound portobello
mushrooms, sliced

½ medium onion, sliced into rings

6 ounces mixed salad greens

11 ounces mandarin
oranges, drained

¼ cup almonds

1. In a small bowl, combine orange juice, olive oil, zest
and a pinch of salt and pepper.

2. In a large, resealable bag add half of the marinade,
mushrooms and onion rings. Seal the bag and rotate to coat
evenly. Let this marinate in the refrigerator for 15 minutes
and set the other half in the refrigerator for later. After
15 minutes, drain the mushrooms and onions and discard
the used marinade.

3. Preheat grill to medium heat and grill the mushrooms
and onions for 8–12 minutes, or until they become tender.
Turn them frequently. Use a grill basket if you have one handy
to make things easier, but don't worry about it otherwise.
Remove from heat when tender and set aside.

4. In a large serving bowl, combine salad greens, oranges,
almonds and the grilled mushrooms and onions. Drizzle with
the remaining marinade and toss to coat. Serve and enjoy.

 ADD MEAT!   Serve this with ½ pound of skinless, boneless chicken breast.
Double the marinade and marinate the chicken for at least 1 hour in a large,
resealable bag in the refrigerator. Grill the pieces for 5–6 minutes on each side,
or until it reaches desired doneness.

Orange Kebabs

Pairing these vegetables with orange may not be the most intuitive thing, but the finished product is sweet enough to be interesting and light enough not to dominate the flavor profile.

1. Begin by making the Spicy Orange Marinade from the "Marinades" chapter.

2. Prepare the kebabs by cutting the onion and oranges into wedges, and then halving the wedges. Thread the vegetables and oranges onto skewers in whichever order you'd like, trying to distribute them as evenly as possible.

3. Marinate the skewers in the Spicy Orange Marinade for about 15 minutes, making sure to baste frequently. Drain and discard the marinade.

4. Preheat grill to medium heat and arrange the kebabs on the grill. Cook the kebabs covered for 10–13 minutes, turning occasionally. Remove from heat when the vegetables have become tender and show slight grill marks. Brush with the orange juice and serve.

1 large yellow onion

1 large navel orange

2 medium bell peppers, cut into ½-inch slices

8 medium cremini mushrooms

10 cherry tomatoes

1 medium summer squash, cut into ½-inch slices

Spicy Orange Marinade ("Marinades & Sauces")

2 tablespoon orange juice

 ADD MEAT! Add steak to the skewers by slicing 1 pound of flank steak into bite-sized cubes. Marinate in the mixture for at least an hour in the refrigerator. Add the cubes to the skewers and grill until they reach desired doneness.

 MAKE IT VEGAN! Replace the butter with olive oil and brush the mixture in the same way.

Vegetable Portobello Caps

ACTIVE TIME: 20 MINUTES • TOTAL TIME: 35 MINUTES • SERVES 4

These caps are marinated in a delicious Italian dressing and really soak up the flavor nicely. They also make the perfect bowl to stuff with chopped and grilled veggies. These are really easy to make and can be marinated in advance.

1. Make the marinade by combining oil, vinegar, garlic, herbs and a pinch of salt. Mix until evenly blended and pour half of the mixture into a large, resealable bag.

2. Prepare the mushrooms by removing and disposing of the stems and gills. Add the mushrooms to the bag and shake to ensure an even coating.

3. In another bag, mix the other half of the marinade with the rest of the vegetables. Let both bags marinate for at least 1 hour in the refrigerator. Drain the vegetables and preheat your grill to medium heat.

4. Place the marinated mushrooms on the grill and cook for 6–8 minutes, flipping once. Grill the rest of the vegetables in a grill basket for 8–12 minutes. Be sure to turn the vegetables frequently while they are grilling.

5. Remove from heat when tender and chop the vegetables into small pieces. Distribute the vegetables between the caps and serve over the mushrooms.

½ cup olive oil

½ cup balsamic vinegar

5 cloves garlic, minced

½ teaspoon dried thyme

½ teaspoon dried basil

½ teaspoon oregano

Salt, to taste

4 large portobello mushrooms

2 medium onions, halved and sliced

2 medium summer squash, halved and sliced

1 bell pepper, cut into ¼-inch slices

2 medium tomatoes, halved and sliced

4 small carrots, quartered

 ADD MEAT! Sprinkle bits of cooked prosciutto into the caps before serving.

Swiss Cheese Romaine Hearts

ACTIVE TIME: 5 MINUTES • TOTAL TIME: 15 MINUTES • SERVES 4

While not as flavorful as my beloved goat cheese, the Swiss is a perfect understated complement to the raspberry vinaigrette.

2 romaine hearts, cut in half lengthwise

1 tablespoon olive oil

Pinch of salt and pepper

⅓ cup Raspberry Vinaigrette ("Marinades & Sauces")

½ cup shredded swiss cheese

½ cup craisins

⅓ cup almonds

1. Preheat your grill to medium heat and lightly oil your grill grates. Brush the romaine halves with oil, season with salt and pepper.

2. Cook the romaine hearts for about 30 seconds on each side, or until they heat through. Transfer them to a platter and drizzle them with vinaigrette, cheese, craisins and almonds. Serve and enjoy.

 ADD MEAT! Serve these with Paleo Pork Chops, found in the "Substitutions" section.

 MAKE IT VEGAN! Remove the cheese from this recipe.

 GO PALEO! Remove the cheese from the recipe and feel free to add Paleo Pork Chops.

Barbecue Mushrooms

ACTIVE TIME: 10 MINUTES • TOTAL TIME: 20 MINUTES • SERVES 4

This is definitely one of the quickest recipes to make! Even though it's simple, it's really delicious and can be accompanied by other veggies, quinoa, rice or even pasta. Add whichever you like best and make it saucy.

24 medium mushrooms

1 cup barbecue sauce

1. Thread the mushrooms onto a skewer and brush with barbecue sauce.

2. Preheat grill to medium heat and place the skewers on the grill. Cook for 10–15 minutes, turning and basting with the remaining barbecue sauce occasionally. Remove from heat when the mushrooms are tender and serve.

 ADD MEAT! Add 12 strips of uncooked bacon. Cut the strips in half and wrap each mushroom with a piece of bacon before grilling. Secure the bacon with a toothpick if necessary. Grill until the bacon is crisp.

 MAKE IT VEGAN! Make sure to use vegan barbecue sauce.

 GO PALEO! Make sure to use paleo barbecue sauce.

 GLUTEN-FREE! Make sure to use gluten-free barbecue sauce.

Raspberry Asparagus

ACTIVE TIME: 10 MINUTES • TOTAL TIME: 20 MINUTES • SERVES 4

Raspberry glaze goes perfectly with this smoky grilled asparagus. I love to have these as a quick snack or for lunch with quinoa!

1. Brush each spear with olive oil and preheat grill to medium heat. Grill the spears for 6–8 minutes, turning once, and remove from heat when asparagus is tender.

2. Heat the jam and balsamic vinegar mixed together in the microwave for 15–20 seconds, or until the jam has melted. Drizzle this mixture over the asparagus and serve.

16 fresh asparagus spears

½ cup raspberry jam

2 tablespoons balsamic vinegar

1 tablespoon olive oil

 ADD MEAT! Add ⅓ pound of thinly sliced prosciutto, cutting the slices in half. Before grilling, wrap each asparagus spear with a piece of prosciutto. Secure with a toothpick if necessary. Grill until the prosciutto is crisp, remove toothpicks and enjoy.

Grilled Nectarines

ACTIVE TIME: 10 MINUTES • TOTAL TIME: 25 MINUTES • SERVES 12

This appetizer is sweet and delicious, takes no time to make and is always a huge hit at barbecues. The balsamic reduction over caramelized nectarines is tough to beat—grill them up and enjoy before the main course.

1. Begin by heating the balsamic vinegar in a small saucepan. Bring it to a boil and cook for about 10–15 minutes, or until it has been reduced to 3 tablespoons. Remove from heat and begin brushing oil over both sides of the bread.

2. Preheat grill to medium heat and grill the slices on both sides until they are golden brown and slightly crispy.

3. Remove the bread and begin grilling the nectarine halves. Grill them on each side for about 1 minute, or until they are lightly browned.

4. Remove the nectarines from heat and spread goat cheese over the toasted slices.

5. Cut the nectarines into slices once they have cooled and add them to the toast. Drizzle them with the reduced balsamic vinegar and sprinkle torn basil over the top. Serve and enjoy.

½ cup balsamic vinegar

1 tablespoon olive oil

12 small slices Italian or French bread

2 medium nectarines, halved

¼ cup goat cheese

Fresh basil leaves, torn

 ADD MEAT! Cook up a few slices of prosciutto and tear over the top of the slices.

 MAKE IT VEGAN! Replace the cheese with one of the vegan options from the "Substitutions" section.

 GO PALEO! Replace the cheese with a paleo option from the supermarket! Use paleo bread as a base.

 GLUTEN-FREE! Use gluten-free bread.

Grilled Plums Topped with Goat Cheese

ACTIVE TIME: 10 MINUTES • TOTAL TIME: 25 MINUTES • SERVES 4

Help your fresh plums reach their full potential by grilling them and pairing them with a bold cheese that can stand up to their sweetness.

1 cup balsamic vinegar

2 teaspoons lemon peel, grated

4 medium firm plums, halved and pitted

½ cup goat cheese, crumbled

1. Begin by heating the balsamic vinegar and lemon zest in a small saucepan. Bring it to a boil and cook for about 10–15 minutes, or until it is reduced to about ⅓ cup.

2. Preheat your grill to medium heat and place the plums on the grill. Cook until the plums become tender, about 2–3 minutes per side.

3. Drizzle glaze and cheese on top and serve.

 ADD MEAT! Serve these with grilled steak. Prepare the steak for grilling by brushing with olive oil and sprinkling with salt and pepper. Grill each side for about 6 minutes for a rare steak, or longer if you prefer a more cooked center. Slice the steak up and drizzle glaze over the pieces.

 MAKE IT VEGAN! Replace the goat cheese with a vegan alternative from the "Substitutions" section.

 GO PALEO! Remove the cheese completely.

Mains

When I was living in a house with six people, I wanted to make meals that elevated simple flavors but still pleased the masses. Naturally, the garden was the perfect place to seek out inspiration. Ranging from quick and easy sandwiches to more elaborate meals, these grilled favorites ensure that you'll never run out of ways to incorporate your favorite homegrown greens into a wholesome dish.

Stuffed Zucchini

Zucchini can be stuffed with just about anything and still taste delicious; I prefer goat cheese for its adaptability, especially when paired with a light, zesty marinara.

4 medium-sized zucchini

15 ounces goat cheese

2 cups marinara sauce

Salt and pepper, to taste

1. Preheat your grill to high heat. Slice your zucchini in half, lengthwise. Hollow out the zucchini by removing seeds, creating a trough. Season the halves with a little salt and pepper.

2. Evenly spread the goat cheese in the troughs of each zucchini, using as little or as much as you'd like. Repeat the process with the marinara sauce.

3. Grill the logs until the cheese becomes soft and the marinara is bubbling slightly. This should take about 10 minutes. Remove from heat and serve.

 ADD MEAT!   Add chopped up ham to the zucchini log when you add the goat cheese.

 MAKE IT VEGAN!   The Moxarella recipe from "Substitutions" will work just as well as the goat cheese.

 GO PALEO!   Use the Paleo Pizza Sauce recipe from "Substitutions" instead of marinara sauce.

Faux Chili— Bean Edition

ACTIVE TIME: 5 MINUTES • TOTAL TIME: 20 MINUTES • SERVES 6

This vegetarian chilli has more protein than you'll know what to do with. Just as importantly, you'll be able to store it easily and eat it all week long.

1 (15-ounce) can black beans

1 (15-ounce) can kidney beans

1 (15-ounce) can pinto beans

1 (15-ounce) can chickpeas

2 ears corn, shucked

½ cup cilantro, chopped

1 jar arrabbiata sauce (about 20 ounces)

1 tablespoon olive oil

1. Drain and rinse all beans and let sit while you prepare the grill. Preheat your grill to medium-high heat.

2. Brush the corn with olive oil and place directly on the grill. Turning the corn, grill for about 8 minutes. Remove from heat and let the corn cool for a bit.

3. Cut the kernels off of the cobs into a small bowl. In a large pot, mix together the beans, corn, cilantro, and arrabbiata sauce.

4. On the grill or the stove, heat until the beans are as tender as you like—approximately 20 minutes. Be sure to mix frequently to properly coat the beans. Remove from heat and serve.

 ADD MEAT! While grilling the corn, grill 1 pound of skinless, boneless chicken breast on medium-high heat for 5 to 6 minutes per side, or until meat is no longer pink. Remove from heat and serve—either on the side or diced and mixed into the chili.

 GO PALEO! Unfortunately beans are not considered paleo. Instead of using beans, find 6 bell peppers and 1 large zucchini. Cut these into ¼-inch strips and grill with the corn. Dice these up and mix them with the corn and sauce after they have reached desired tenderness.

Stuffed Bell Peppers

Not only are these peppers delicious, but also easy to make and filled with fiber and protein. These can be prepared as either a main dish or as a side. As a time saver, feel free to use white rice instead.

1. Begin by cooking your brown rice according to package instructions. Let cool while preparing your bell peppers.

2. Cut bell peppers in half lengthwise and remove the seeds.

3. In a large bowl, mix the beans (rinsed and drained), rice, onions, cilantro, vegetable oil, lime juice, garlic and a pinch of salt.

4. Preheat your grill to medium heat and cut a piece of foil large enough to fully surround the peppers. Spray one side of the foil with cooking spray.

5. Place the peppers on the foil and evenly fill with the bean mixture. Cover each pepper with its other half so the edges meet. Seal the foil edges by making two tight folds. Place packets on the grill and let cook until the peppers become tender, about 15–20 minutes.

6. After opening the packets, sprinkle your diced tomato over the peppers and serve.

3 large bell peppers
(colors of your choosing)

1 (16 ounce) can of black beans

½ cup brown rice

4 medium green
onions, chopped

¼ cup cilantro, finely chopped

2 tablespoons vegetable oil

2 tablespoons lime juice

1 clove garlic, minced

1 plum tomato, diced

Salt, to taste

 ADD MEAT! Cook 1 pound of ground mild sausage seasoned with garlic and chili powder. Bring the heat down to low and add frozen corn along with the remaining mixture ingredients. The result will be delightfully savory—and filling to boot.

 GO PALEO! Since black beans are not paleo, remove them from the recipe and double the number of bell peppers.

 GLUTEN-FREE! Brown rice is not gluten-free, so switch to white rice instead and cook according to package instructions. Quinoa will also work well.

Kale and Feta Pita Pizza

ACTIVE TIME: 10 MINUTES • TOTAL TIME: 15 MINUTES • SERVES 4

These days, you can find these Turkish pizzas at plenty of markets, but it's much more satisfying to make them yourself.

1. Mix the olive oil, onion, garlic, kale, feta, cheddar and a pinch of paprika in a large bowl. Be sure to mix well.

2. Spread about half of the mixture over one of the pita breads and place another pita on top. Repeat this with the other half of the filling on the other two pieces of pita. Preheat your grill to medium-high heat.

3. Before placing the pizza on the grill, brush the exposed pita side with olive oil. Grill these for about 3–4 minutes or until they begin to crisp and turn a nice golden color. Compress with a metal spatula.

4. While these cook, cut lemons into wedges. Remove from heat when pitas reach desired crispness and serve in wedges. Squeeze lemon over the pita for a bit more flavor.

1 tablespoon of olive oil

1 red onion (finely chopped)

2 cloves of garlic (minced)

6 ounces kale (finely shredded)

7 ounces feta cheese (crumbled)

½ cup cheddar cheese (shredded)

Pinch of paprika

4 Greek pita breads (approximately 10 inches across)

2 lemons

 ADD MEAT!   Add slices of torn cooked ham to the top of the pita breads before cooking. They should crisp up nicely while grilling.

 MAKE IT VEGAN!   Remove cheese from the recipe and instead top with 1 diced bell pepper for extra flavor. Feel free to use vegan shredded cheese as well.

  GO PALEO AND GLUTEN-FREE!   Use the Paleo Pizza Dough (page 15) and Gluten-Free Pizza Dough (page 14) respectively.

Curry Vegetables

ACTIVE TIME: 5 MINUTES • TOTAL TIME: 20 MINUTES • SERVES 4

The curry powder gives the vegetables a unique, earthy flavor, and the mixture of herbs works wonderfully with the zucchini and peppers.

1 medium zucchini

2 bell peppers

1 tablespoon olive oil

2 teaspoon curry powder

½ cup cooked chickpeas

Cilantro leaves

1 tablespoon crumbled feta, for garnish

1. Preheat your grill to medium heat and slice zucchini and bell peppers into strips. Brush both sides of the vegetables with olive oil and sprinkle curry powder over them.

2. Grill each side for 3–5 minutes, or until the vegetables become tender and lightly charred.

3. Remove from heat and chop. Toss with the cooked chickpeas and garnish with feta and torn cilantro leaves.

 ADD MEAT! Grill 1 pound of skinless, boneless chicken breast. Rub the chicken with curry powder and grill for 5–6 minutes per side, or until fully cooked through.

 MAKE IT VEGAN! Simply remove the feta cheese.

 GO PALEO! Remove the cheese and chickpeas. Serve over ½ cup of cooked white rice, a "safe starch," or use the Cauliflower Rice ("Substitutions" chapter).

Curry Asparagus over Rice

ACTIVE TIME: 10 MINUTES • TOTAL TIME: 20 MINUTES • SERVES 4

Asparagus is one of the best vegetables to grill. It's very simple and can be made however you like. When served over brown rice this meal has tons of fiber and protein.

1 cup brown rice

1 bunch asparagus

½ cup olive oil

2 teaspoons curry powder

½ teaspoon cumin

Pinch of crushed red pepper, to taste

½ cup mint leaves, dry

Salt and pepper, to taste

1. Begin by cooking brown rice as instructed on the packaging.

2. While your rice is cooking, rinse and dry the asparagus. Place in a resealable bag and add olive oil to coat.

3. Whisk together curry powder, cumin, red pepper, mint leaves, salt and pepper, adding this mixture to the bag. Mix until all asparagus is evenly coated.

4. Preheat your grill to medium heat and begin grilling when rice has 5 minutes remaining. Grill the coated asparagus for 10 minutes, rotating at least once. Remove from heat and serve over rice.

 ADD MEAT! Wrap uncooked bacon around the asparagus. Secure with a toothpick if necessary and grill until the asparagus is tender and the bacon is crisp.

 GO PALEO! Instead of brown rice, check out my recipe for Cauliflower Rice in the "Substitutions" chapter.

 GLUTEN-FREE! Serve over cooked white rice instead of brown rice.

Eggplant Rollatini

ACTIVE TIME: 25 MINUTES • TOTAL TIME: 35 MINUTES • SERVING SIZE: 4

This recipe takes a bit more time than the others, but it's definitely worth it if you're looking for something new and delicious to try.

1. Slice eggplant lengthwise to yield 12 slices. Place the slices in a colander and salt them.

2. After letting the slices drain for 20 minutes, dry and coat them in olive oil, salt and pepper.

3. Preheat grill to medium heat. Grill the slices for 10 minutes, flipping them over halfway through. Cook your slices until grill marks appear and they become slightly tender. Remove from heat and allow them to cool.

4. In a medium-sized bowl, mix together the ricotta, lemon zest, basil, nutmeg and as much Parmesan as you want.

5. Once everything is properly mixed, lay out your eggplant slices. Add a few tablespoons of the mixture to the end closest to you. Roll up the eggplant and secure it with a toothpick.

6. Grill the eggplant for about 2 more minutes, remove from heat and serve.

3 regular eggplants (about 8 inches)

½ cup olive oil

1½ cups ricotta

Zest of ½ lemon

1 tablespoon basil, chopped

Nutmeg, freshly grated

Parmesan cheese, to taste

Pinch of salt and pepper, to taste

 ADD MEAT! Bacon bits make a great addition to your cheesy spread.

 MAKE IT VEGAN! Make this paleo by replacing the ricotta cheese with the Macadamia Ricotta Cheese from "Substitutions."

 GO PALEO! As it's both vegan and paleo, swap in the Macadamia Ricotta Cheese from "Substitutions."

Broccoli over Rice

ACTIVE TIME: 10 MINUTES • TOTAL TIME: 30 MINUTES • SERVES 4

This is a super easy recipe that's perfect on those nights where you don't know what to make and want something easy and delicious. Zucchini is easily substituted with any squash of your choosing.

1. Cook rice according to package instructions. Once cooked, let it sit while preparing zucchini.

2. Remove the broccoli florets from the heads and cut into small pieces. Next, toss the pieces in a large bowl with oil and soy sauce.

3. Preheat grill to medium-high heat and cook zucchini for about 3 minutes per side. Remove from heat and cut into cubes. If you want, whip up the Lemon Vinaigrette ("Marinades & Sauces") and drizzle over; otherwise, serve over rice as is.

1 cup brown rice
2 medium broccoli heads
1 tablespoon olive oil
1 tablespoon soy sauce
Lemon Vinaigrette (optional)

 ADD MEAT! Serve with cooked bacon bits sprinkled over the zucchini and rice.

 GO PALEO! Serve over Cauliflower Rice ("Substitutions"). Instead of soy sauce, use coconut aminos.

 GLUTEN-FREE! Serve over white rice instead.

Grilled Veggie Pasta

ACTIVE TIME: 10 MINUTES • TOTAL TIME: 25 MINUTES • SERVES 4

Pasta with fresh, grilled vegetables is a thing of beauty. The vegetables in this recipe can easily be swapped for the ones that you most prefer.

2 small zucchini

1 small yellow squash

3 medium tomatoes

1 red bell pepper

1 small white onion

2 cloves garlic, minced

2 tablespoon olive oil

Pinch of salt and pepper, to taste

7 ounces pasta, cooked

¼ cup basil, chopped

½ cup Parmesan cheese, grated

Paleo Pizza Sauce (optional)

1. Begin by cutting the zucchini and yellow squash in half, lengthwise. Cut the tomatoes, red bell pepper and onion into 1-inch slices.

2. In a large bowl, toss the zucchini, yellow squash, tomatoes, bell pepper, onion, garlic and olive oil. Add salt and pepper. Ensure that all vegetables are evenly coated.

3. Preheat your grill to medium-high heat. Place everything on the grill and cook until they become tender, about 5–6 minutes. To keep the onion together while grilling, place a skewer through the center.

4. Once tender, remove from grill and let cool slightly. Cut the vegetables into bite-sized cubes.

5. Place cooked, drained pasta in a large serving bowl, add cubes and basil and toss until adequately mixed. Sprinkle cheese on top and serve. If you're looking for a sauce recommendation, the Paleo Pizza Sauce makes a great addition to the dish!

 ADD MEAT! Grill up some flank steak. Prepare the steak for grilling. Grill each side for about 6 minutes (rare), or until desired tenderness. Dice and add to your bowl.

 MAKE IT VEGAN! Simply remove the cheese. Replace with Vegan Parmesan Cheese from "Substitutions," or don't! This tastes just as great without the cheese.

 GO PALEO! Remove the pasta and serve over 2 cups of fresh salad greens.

 GLUTEN-FREE! Serve over gluten-free pasta, or just use salad greens like our paleo friends!

Eggplant Ratatouille

The best part about this ratatouille is that it already accommodates most diets. It takes a bit longer to make than some of the other recipes, but the smokiness it retains from the grill makes this dish worth the wait.

1 cup brown rice

1 medium eggplant

1 medium summer squash

1 medium zucchini

1 medium onion

1 can stewed tomatoes

¼ cup parsley

¼ cup basil leaves

3 tablespoons olive oil

2 cloves garlic, minced

Pinch of dried basil, oregano, salt and pepper

1. Cook brown rice according to package directions. Prepare vegetables by cutting eggplant into ½-inch pieces, the summer squash and zucchini in half lengthwise, and onions into quarters. Wash the eggplant pieces and sprinkle with salt. Let sit for 30 minutes.

2. In a large bowl, pour 2 tablespoons of olive oil. Add eggplant, squash, zucchini and onion to the bowl and toss to coat. Preheat grill to medium-high heat. Place eggplant, squash, and zucchini directly on the grill. Skewer the onions before placing on the grill. Grill vegetables until they are lightly charred: about 10-12 minutes for the onions, and 4-5 minutes per side for the eggplant, squash, and zucchini. Remove from heat and let cool.

3. Cut the eggplant into cubes and the squash and zucchini into slivers. Add 1 tablespoon of olive oil to a large saucepan and then cook over low heat until the garlic is golden, about 2 minutes. Stir in the grilled vegetables, stewed tomatoes, parsley, dried basil, oregano, salt and pepper. Cook for about 30 minutes. Stir in the basil leaves and then serve over brown rice.

 ADD MEAT! Sear pieces of top round beef cut into bite-sized pieces brushed in olive oil until they become golden brown. Add this to the saucepan.

 GO PALEO! Serve over Cauliflower Rice (from the "Substitutions" chapter) instead of brown. You can also serve this over white rice if you're okay with white rice as a "safe starch."

 GLUTEN-FREE! Serve over quinoa or white rice instead of brown rice. Cook according to package directions.

Cucumber and Avocado Sandwich

ACTIVE TIME: 15 MINUTES • TOTAL TIME: 20 MINUTES • SERVES 2

Another summer favorite that can be adjusted to fit everyone's needs. This is a super simple recipe that will help you get out of that sandwich rut. Try this out with tea or fresh lemonade, and enjoy.

1. Begin by washing and drying the spinach, peeling and slicing the cucumber and peeling, pitting, and slicing the avocado.

2. Spread goat cheese evenly on all bread slices. On two slices of the bread, top with spinach, cucumber, and avocado slices. Drizzle some lemon juice over cucumbers and avocado slices. Add sprouts and season with salt and pepper. Place the other slices of bread on top, goat cheese side down.

3. Preheat grill to medium heat. Grill sandwiches for about 2 minutes per side, remove from heat and serve.

4 slices whole grain bread
4 ounces goat cheese
1 handful spinach leaves
½ large cucumber
1 large avocado
2 teaspoons lemon juice
½ cup alfalfa sprouts
Salt and pepper, to taste

 ADD MEAT! Add slices of deli ham to the sandwich, cooked or uncooked.

 MAKE IT VEGAN! Remove cheese from the sandwich and enjoy as is.

 GO PALEO! Remove the cheese from the sandwich and swap out the bread for any paleo bread.

 GLUTEN-FREE! Swap out the bread with gluten-free bread, which can be found in most supermarkets.

Grilled Zucchini Wrap

ACTIVE TIME: 5 MINUTES • TOTAL TIME: 20 MINUTES • SERVES 4

Making a vegetable wrap is a great way of ensuring that all of your favorite ingredients go into a dish. As such, I encourage you to play with your favorite vegetable combinations here.

Zucchini, cut into ¼-inch-thick strips

1 red bell pepper, cut into ½-inch strips

1 small yellow squash, cut into ¼-inch-thick strips

1 tablespoon olive oil and ½ teaspoon olive oil (separate)

1 cup baby spinach

1 (15-ounce) can white beans

1 clove garlic, minced

4 8-inch tortillas

Fresh basil leaves

Salt and pepper, to taste

1. In a large bowl, toss together zucchini, bell pepper, squash, and 1 tablespoon of olive oil. Season with salt and pepper.

2. Preheat grill to medium heat and grill the zucchini, bell pepper and squash for 4–6 minutes per side, flipping once.

3. In a medium bowl, mash together the beans, garlic and ½ teaspoon olive oil until the mixture becomes smooth.

4. Spread the bean mixture evenly over the 4 tortillas and top each with a few fresh basil leaves.

5. Slice the grilled vegetables into thin slices and distribute them evenly over the tortillas. Add the baby spinach and roll the wrap using your preferred method. Cut the wraps in half and serve.

 ADD MEAT!   Grill 1 pound of skinless, boneless chicken breast before preparing the tortillas. Grill them for 5–6 minutes per side, or until they're cooked through. Dice the grilled chicken and distribute the pieces between the tortillas!

 GO PALEO!   Make this a salad by removing the wrap and tossing the vegetables with lemon juice and olive oil. Feel free to add grilled chicken as well.

 GLUTEN-FREE!   Use Paleo Tortillas from "Substitutions," or make it a salad instead.

Grilled Zucchini Parm

ACTIVE TIME: 15 MINUTES • TOTAL TIME: 20 MINUTES • SERVES 4

This is a fun way to utilize your summer squash and add a bit of Italian flavor to these zucchini rounds.

3 medium zucchini

1 tablespoon of olive oil

2 tablespoons of butter, softened

2 cloves of garlic, minced

1 tablespoon parsley, chopped

½ cup Parmesan cheese, grated

Salt, to taste

Preheat grill to medium-high heat. Oil the grill to prevent sticking. Cut each zucchini lengthwise into four pieces. In a small bowl, mix together the olive oil, butter, garlic and parsley. Add a pinch of salt to the mixture, to taste. Use this mixture to coat the zucchini slices. Place these on the hot grates and grill until the slices are tender. This should take about 8 minutes. Sprinkle one side of the zucchini with Parmesan cheese. Remove from heat and serve.

 ADD MEAT! Add chicken or use it as a replacement for the zucchini. Coat 1 pound of skinless, boneless chicken in the same way you'd coat the zucchini and grill for 5–6 minutes per side, or until it is completely cooked through. Top with mozzarella cheese and cook until cheese melts.

 MAKE IT VEGAN! Use Moxarella or Vegan Parmesan Cheese from "Substitutions." Replace the butter with 1½ tablespoons of olive oil.

 GO PALEO! Use the Vegan Parmesan Cheese recipe from "Substitutions."

Thai Tofu and Eggplant

ACTIVE TIME: 15 MINUTES • TOTAL TIME: 35 MINUTES • SERVES 4

Thai food is truly one of the greatest things around. With such unique and amazing flavors you really can't go wrong. When making this, be sure to let the soy sauce sink into the tofu for maximum flavor!

1. Cook basmati rice according to package instructions and let sit while preparing the rest of the dish.

2. Preheat grill to high heat. Slice the eggplant lengthwise and grill for 8–10 minutes, or until all sides are slightly charred. Let these cool to the side.

3. In a food processor, combine the red peppers, garlic, onion, sugar and lime juice. Mix until it becomes smooth.

4. In a large skillet, heat the oil and add the processed mixture. Cook for 1 minute on medium heat.

5. Drizzle soy sauce on tofu. Add the tofu, grilled eggplant and half of the basil to the skillet. Cook until they are sufficiently heated through.

6. Remove and serve with over rice, using the remaining basil leaves for garnish.

1 cup basmati rice
1 large eggplant
3 red peppers, sliced
4 cloves garlic, minced
1 small onion, cut into quarters
3 teaspoons brown sugar
2 tablespoons lime juice
1 tablespoon vegetable oil
8 ounces tofu, diced
1 teaspoon soy sauce
¼ cup basil leaves

 ADD MEAT! Replace tofu with 1 pound of skinless, boneless chicken breast cut into cubes.

 GO PALEO! Replace soy sauce with coconut aminos.

Eggplant Sandwiches

ACTIVE TIME: 20 MINUTES • TOTAL TIME: 35 MINUTES • SERVES 4

Grilled eggplant is super versatile and I especially like it in sandwich form. This recipe is really easy to adjust to fit dietary restrictions. The olive spread tastes wonderful with the grilled veggies and really enhances this sandwich.

1. Begin by placing the olives, balsamic vinegar, red wine vinegar, 1 clove garlic and a pinch of salt and pepper in a food processor. While processing, add ¼ cup of olive oil and process the mixture until it has blended evenly. Set this aside for later use.

2. In a small bowl, mix together ¼ cup of olive oil, 3 cloves of garlic and a pinch of salt and pepper. Mix this until evenly blended and brush the mixture over the eggplant and bell peppers.

3. Preheat your grill to medium heat and place the vegetables on a grill rack or in a grill basket. Grill for 10–12 minutes, covered. Remove from heat when vegetables have become tender, and grill the bread for about 2 minutes.

4. Assemble your sandwiches by spreading the olive mixture over the bread and topping with eggplant, peppers, a sprinkle of basil and another slice of bread. Serve and enjoy.

½ cup pitted olives

2 tablespoons balsamic vinegar

2 teaspoons red wine vinegar

4 cloves garlic, minced

Salt and pepper, to taste

½ cup olive oil

1 large eggplant, cut lengthwise into ¼-inch slices

2 bell peppers, quartered

8 slices whole grain bread

6 fresh basil leaves, torn

 ADD MEAT! Add slices of ham, turkey, or prosciutto to this sandwich.

 GO PALEO! Replace the bread with paleo bread from your local supermarket.

 GLUTEN-FREE! Replace the bread with gluten-free bread from your local supermarket.

Grilled Vegetable Pasta with Feta

ACTIVE TIME: 10 MINUTES • TOTAL TIME: 25 MINUTES • SERVES 4

Being Italian, I basically have pasta running through my veins. That's probably why I love to make pasta topped with vegetables for just about every meal!

10 ounces feta cheese, cubed in oil with herbs and spices

3 bell peppers, color of your choosing

1 large red onion

12 ounces cherry tomatoes

2 tablespoons oregano, chopped

1 pound penne pasta

Salt and pepper, to taste

1. Cook pasta according to package directions.

2. Slice the bell peppers into ¾-inch-thick strips and red onion into ¾-inch-thick wedges.

3. In a large bowl, drain all herb and spices from feta cheese. Add the bell peppers, onions and cherry tomatoes to marinate in the herbs and spices. Toss to coat, adding salt and pepper.

4. Thread the tomatoes, peppers, and onion wedges onto separate skewers since their cooking times will vary. Grill vegetables until they are lightly charred: about 15 minutes for the onions, 10 minutes for the peppers, and 5 minutes for the tomatoes.

5. In a large bowl, toss together pasta, grilled vegetables, oregano and feta. Season with salt and pepper and serve.

 ADD MEAT! Grill up a few pieces of skinless, boneless chicken breast (about 1 pound) over medium heat for 5–6 minutes per side, or until cooked thoroughly. Remove from heat, dice and add to the pasta.

 MAKE IT VEGAN! Instead of feta, use the Moxarella recipe in "Substitutions," or remove cheese entirely. It'll still taste great without it.

 GO PALEO! Instead of serving this over pasta, serve it over Cauliflower Rice (from the "Substitutions" chapter) or a bed of greens. Remove the cheese.

 GLUTEN-FREE! Cook up some gluten-free pasta, which can be found in most supermarkets.

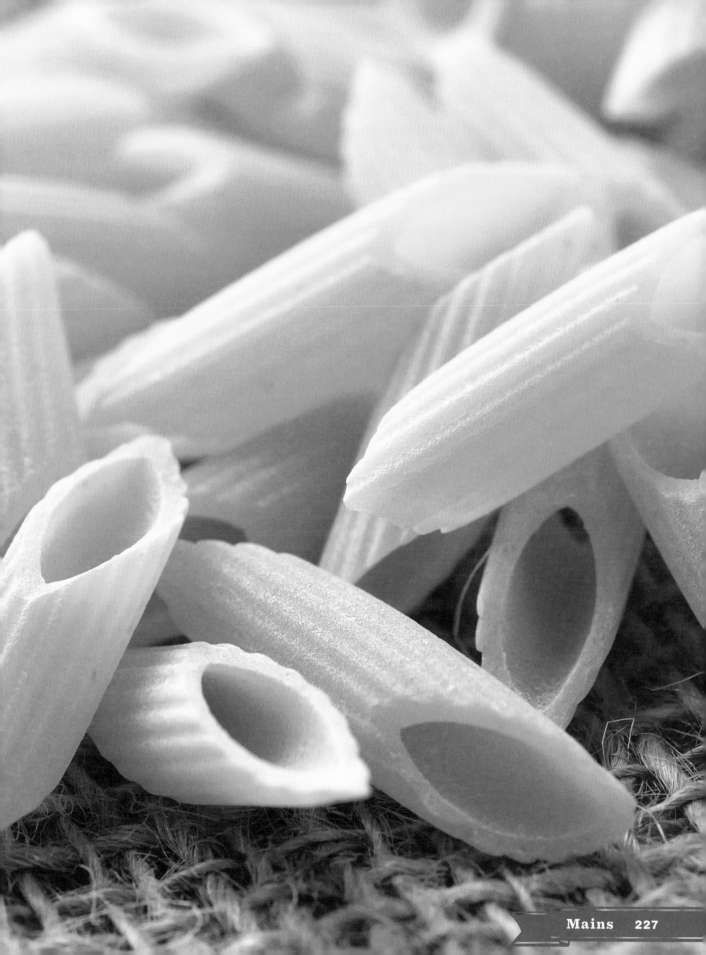

Grilled Vegetables over Orzo

ACTIVE TIME: 20 MINUTES • TOTAL TIME: 40 MINUTES • SERVES 6

Foil packets are used in many of these recipes because the of the simple prep time, concentrated flavors and easy cleanup. These are a huge hit at my house!

1 medium eggplant

2 bell peppers, color
of your choosing

1 red onion

2 cloves garlic, minced

⅓ cup olive oil

Salt and pepper, to taste

1 cup orzo

⅓ cup lemon juice

⅓ cup olive oil, for dressing

¼ cup pine nuts

¾ pound feta, crumbled

6 fresh basil leaves, torn

1. Preheat grill to medium-high heat. Peel and dice all vegetables, creating 1-inch cubes.

2. In a large bowl, toss eggplant, bell peppers, onion, garlic, olive oil, salt and pepper.

3. Cut 2 large pieces of foil and spread the tossed vegetables over one piece of foil. Cover this with the other piece and crimp the edges, making a sealed packet. Place packet on grill and cook for about 15–20 minutes, or until vegetables become tender.

4. In the meantime, cook the orzo in boiling salted water until tender. This should take 7–9 minutes.

5. After the orzo is fully cooked, strain and transfer to a large serving bowl. Mix in the vegetables from the foil packet into the serving bowl, making sure to transfer the herbs and juices as well. Once the mixture has cooled add pine nuts and crumbled feta on top.

 ADD MEAT! Add 1 pound of meat (chicken, beef, or whatever else you'd like!) and dice it into 1½-inch cubes. Toss to coat with olive oil and add the cubes to the foil packets. Cook until it has reached desired doneness. It might be easier to cook meat in a separate packet to ensure that it is fully cooked.

 MAKE IT VEGAN! Remove or replace the feta cheese with a vegan substitute from "Substitutions."

 GO PALEO! Replace the feta cheese with a paleo substitute from "Substitutions."

Quinoa Veggie Wraps

Layers of texture and flavor make this wrap an easy crowd-pleaser. Be sure to save the leftover mixture for later use.

1 large red onion

2 large bell peppers (color is based on your preference)

1 medium zucchini

1 medium eggplant

2 medium tomatoes

½ cup olive oil

2 tablespoons balsamic vinegar

1 clove garlic, minced

1 teaspoon thyme, dried

Salt and pepper, to taste

2 ears of corn, shucked

3 cups quinoa, cooked according to package instructions

2 tablespoon parsley, chopped

1 tablespoon mint, chopped

Lemon juice

5 large tortillas

1. Slice all of the veggies into approximately same-sized pieces.

2. In a large bowl, combine the slices of onion, peppers, zucchini, eggplant and tomato. Toss with balsamic vinegar, olive oil, garlic and thyme. Add a pinch of salt and pepper and let your veggies marinate for about an hour.

3. Preheat your grill to medium heat. Cut 2 large pieces of foil and spread the tossed vegetables over one piece of foil. Cover this with the other piece and crimp the edges, making a sealed packet. Place packet on grill and cook for about 15–20 minutes, or until vegetables become tender. Cutting the slices to approximately the same sizes will help ensure similar cooking times.

4. Meanwhile, brush the ears of corn with olive oil and place them directly on the grill. Turn the corn and grill for about 8 minutes, or until corn becomes lightly charred. Once the corn is properly tender, remove from heat and set aside to let cool.

5. Add cooked quinoa to a large serving bowl. Once the corn is cool, cut the kernels from the cob and add to the serving bowl with the parsley and mint.

6. Once your veggie packet has been properly cooked, remove from heat and chop the vegetables into bite-sized pieces, adding to the serving bowl. Toss the bowl's contents and drizzle in olive oil and a bit of lemon juice. Add salt and ground pepper, to taste.

7. Take the quinoa-vegetable mixture and distribute it evenly between the tortillas. Wrap the tortillas by folding in two edges and rolling tightly. Slice and serve.

 ADD MEAT!   Grill 1 pound of skinless, boneless chicken breast over medium heat for 5–6 minutes per side, or until it is completely cooked through. Chop the chicken into bite-sized pieces and add it to the quinoa-vegetable mixture.

 GO PALEO!   Make the Paleo Tortillas from "Substitutions" and replace quinoa with the Cauliflower Rice!

 GLUTEN-FREE!   Make the Paleo Tortillas from "Substitutions."

Grilled Corn Medley

ACTIVE TIME: 20 MINUTES • TOTAL TIME: 30 MINUTES • SERVES 4

Corn, beans and rice: deliciously simple, and the perfect meal to save when you're too busy to make a new lunch every day.

1 cup orzo

2 ears corn, shucked

12 cherry tomatoes, halved

2 green onions, roots trimmed

1 (15-ounce) can black beans

¼ cup buttermilk

3 tablespoons cilantro

3 tablespoons lime juice

2 tablespoons sour cream

½ teaspoon chili powder

½ teaspoon salt

¼ teaspoon pepper

¼ teaspoon red pepper, ground

2 cloves garlic, minced

1 avocado, peeled and pitted

1. Begin by cooking orzo according to package instructions. Drain, rinse and set aside.

2. Preheat grill to medium heat and brush the ears of corn and sliced onion with oil. Place the two ears of corn and green onions directly on the grill. Grill the green onions for 1–2 minutes, or until they have softened. Making sure to turn regularly, grill the corn for about 8 minutes or until corn becomes lightly charred. Let these cool for a bit.

3. When everything has cooled, cut the kernels from the cob into a large bowl. Add orzo, tomatoes, onions and black beans to the bowl. Toss and let sit.

4. In a small bowl, mix together buttermilk, cilantro, lime juice, sour cream, chili powder, salt, pepper, red onion and garlic. This will be your dressing. Be sure to stir well with a whisk.

5. Chop the avocado into bite-sized pieces and coat with dressing. Drizzle the dressing over the orzo mixture and top with the lightly dressed avocado. Serve and enjoy.

 ADD MEAT! Prepare 1¼ pounds of skirt steak by seasoning with salt and pepper. Grill for 5 minutes per side, or until it reaches desired doneness! Serve sliced over the salad.

 MAKE IT VEGAN! Remove the buttermilk and sour cream from the recipe.

 GO PALEO! Remove the buttermilk and sour cream from the recipe! Remove the black beans and add grass-fed beef for extra protein.

 GLUTEN-FREE! Use white rice instead of orzo.

Grilled Eggplant Sandwich

ACTIVE TIME: 15 MINUTES • TOTAL TIME: 25 MINUTES • SERVES 4

These familiar flavors will help you feel wholesome and clean—especially without the heaviness of the bread.

1 medium eggplant, cut into ¼-inch rounds

3 medium tomatoes, sliced

15 ounces goat cheese

Fresh basil leaves

4 tablespoons olive oil

2 tablespoons balsamic vinegar

Salt and pepper, to taste

1. Preheat your grill to medium heat. Toss eggplant rounds in olive oil, balsamic vinegar, salt and pepper.

2. Grill the eggplant slices for about 7–8 minutes per side, or until lightly charred. Remove from heat.

3. Top half of the eggplant slices with goat cheese, basil leaf, and a slice of tomato. Lightly sprinkle salt and pepper and top with remaining eggplant slices. To secure your mini sandwich, use a toothpick.

 ADD MEAT! Add two strips of cooked bacon to each sandwich.

 MAKE IT VEGAN! Replace cheese with Macadamia Ricotta Cheese from "Substitutions," which can easily be made in a food processor.

 GO PALEO! Use the same steps as the vegan section to make this paleo.

Goat Cheese Eggplant Rollatini

ACTIVE TIME: 10 MINUTES • TOTAL TIME: 20 MINUTES • SERVES 4

This is a fantastic alternative to a traditional rollatini, forgoing the in order to let the eggplant shine on its own.

1. Slice eggplant into ¼-inch-thick pieces, lengthwise. Lay the slices on paper towels and sprinkle generously with salt. Let these sit for 20–30 minutes, or until beads of water form on the surface. Remove salt by rinsing with cold water and patting the slices dry.

2. Preheat grill to medium heat and brush one side of each slice with olive oil. Place the eggplant on the grill oiled side down and cook until grill marks appear and eggplant softens slightly. Brush the tops with oil and flip, once again grilling until they are slightly browned. This should take about 2 minutes per side.

3. Transfer these to a large plate or platter and arrange in a single layer. Scatter chives, sprinkle balsamic vinegar, and thyme over the tops of the slices. Let these stand for a few minutes.

4. Spread goat cheese over the slices and roll them up into a tight spiral. Secure with a toothpick and serve.

1 eggplant
½ cup olive oil
⅓ cup chives, chopped
1 teaspoon balsamic vinegar
12 thyme leaves, finely chopped
15 ounces goat cheese

 ADD MEAT! You can add meat by wrapping a slice of uncooked bacon around each roll and grilling until the bacon becomes crisp.

 MAKE IT VEGAN! Replace the cheese with Moxarella from "Substitutions."

 GO PALEO! Remove the cheese and replace it with Macadamia Ricotta Cheese from "Substitutions."

Grilled Pita Pocket

ACTIVE TIME: 10 MINUTES • TOTAL TIME: 20 MINUTES • SERVES 4

This quick and simple recipe utilizes fresh vegetables and goat cheese to really stand out. Pita pockets are delicious and easy to find, giving your sandwich a little something extra. I also like that it keeps the contents of my sandwich inside, rather than all over the plate.

2 tablespoons olive oil

2 bell peppers

1 medium zucchini

1 small red onion

1 large avocado

15 ounces goat cheese, crumbled

4 small pita breads

1 cup arugula

1. Cut onions into small wedges, and all other vegetables into $1/4$-inch-thick strips. Preheat grill to medium heat.

2. Cut the avocado into thin slices. Set aside.

3. Brush the bell peppers, zucchini and onions with olive oil. Place them on the grill and cook until they become tender—about 5 minutes on each side. Check for slight grill marks, remove from heat and set aside.

4. Cut the pita pockets in half in order to create open spaces for your vegetables. Evenly distribute the grilled vegetables, avocado slices, goat cheese and arugula into the pitas.

5. Place these on the grill for 2 minutes, flipping halfway. Once the cheese has melted slightly and grill marks begin to appear, remove from heat and serve.

 ADD MEAT! Add a few slices of turkey to the sandwich; heated or unheated, the deli meat will taste great in this sandwich!

 MAKE IT VEGAN! Replace the goat cheese with Moxarella from "Substitutions."

 GO PALEO! Remove the cheese from this and use paleo bread.

 GLUTEN-FREE! Use gluten-free pita pockets or bread.

Vegetable Hummus Wraps

ACTIVE TIME: 10 MINUTES • TOTAL TIME: 15 MINUTES • SERVES 4

Packed with vegetables and wonderful hummus, these veggie wraps are sure to make everyone happy.

4 (½-inch-thick) slices red onion

1 bell pepper, any color

1 medium eggplant

2 tablespoon olive oil

¼ cup fresh parsley, chopped

⅛ teaspoon salt

1 (8-ounce) container plain hummus

4 medium whole-grain tortillas

½ cup feta cheese, crumbled

1. Seed the bell pepper and cut into quarters. Cut your eggplant into ½-inch-thick slices.

2. Using 1 tablespoon of olive oil, brush to coat onion, bell pepper and eggplant.

3. Heat your grill to medium-high heat. Grill onion, bell pepper and eggplant for 4 minutes per side, or until tender. Remove from heat and chop vegetables into thin slices.

4. In a medium bowl, combine vegetables, 1 tablespoon of oil, parsley, and salt. Toss to coat and combine.

5. Lay out your tortillas and spread hummus over them. Spread as much or as little as you like. Leave a slight border around the edges to keep hummus from spilling out.

6. Evenly divide the vegetables over the tortillas and top with cheese. Roll up the wraps tightly, cut in half, and serve.

ADD MEAT!   Add beef or chicken to this recipe easily. Grill up 1 ½ pounds of skinless, boneless chicken breast for 5–6 minutes per side or until it reaches desired doneness. Slice the meat up and throw it in your wrap for extra protein and flavor.

 MAKE IT VEGAN!   Replace the feta with one of the vegan cheeses from "Substitutions."

 GO PALEO!   Since chickpeas aren't paleo, the hummus will have to go. You can find some paleo-friendly sweet potato hummus in select stores, but this wrap is still good without it. Additionally, replace the cheese with Macadamia Ricotta or just remove it completely. And don't forget to use Paleo Tortillas as well, unless you'd prefer to turn this into a salad by serving it over 2 cups of greens.

 GLUTEN-FREE!   Use Paleo Tortillas from "Substitutions."

Grilled Spaghetti Squash

ACTIVE TIME: 15 MINUTES • **TOTAL TIME: 45 MINUTES** • **SERVES 4**

Spaghetti squash is like pasta without the guilt. This grilled favorite will be a useful alternative to those looking to cut down on carbs.

2 large spaghetti squash, fully yellow

2 tablespoons olive oil

Salt and pepper, to taste

1 teaspoon paprika

Parmesan cheese, for garnish

1. Prepare spaghetti squash by slicing them in half lengthwise and scooping out the seeds. Brush olive oil on the flesh to ensure an even coating. Sprinkle salt, pepper and paprika on top.

2. Preheat your grill to medium-high heat and place the squash halves flesh side up on the hot grill. Grill for 25–30 minutes, covered, and test for desired tenderness with a fork. If the squash is soft then it's ready! Feel free to add extra seasoning and Parmesan cheese as it cools slightly.

3. Once the squash is cool enough, flesh out the "spaghetti" with a fork and serve.

 ADD MEAT! This is delicious with a meat sauce, found at any supermarket.

 MAKE IT VEGAN! Remove the Parmesan cheese and replace it with Vegan Parmesan from "Substitutions."

 GO PALEO! Remove the Parmesan cheese and replace it with Vegan Parmesan from "Substitutions." If you want, you can top it with a paleo meat sauce as well.

Grilled Veggie Quesadillas

ACTIVE TIME: 20 MINUTES • TOTAL TIME: 40 MINUTES • SERVING SIZE: 4

This veggie-packed dish is the perfect dinner for a nice summer night. Whip up these delicious quesadillas and make the whole family happy.

1. Preheat your grill to medium heat. Begin by seasoning your zucchini with salt and pepper. When slicing the peppers, be sure to remove the seeds.

2. Grill the vegetables until they become slightly soft and charred. Bell peppers should take about 8 to 10 minutes, zucchini about 8.

3. On a separate plate, add 2 tablespoons of pesto to one of the quesadillas. Add about ¼ of the grilled veggies to the quesadilla and then add ¼ cup of goat cheese. Fold the quesadilla in half (forming a half circle). Repeat this process with the remaining tortillas.

4. When you're done, grill the folded quesadillas for about 3 minutes on each side. Remove from heat, cut into wedges and serve. If you want a little extra flavor, try the Peachy Paleo Salsa with these!

4 large tortillas

2 large green zucchini, cut into ¼-inch slices

2 large yellow zucchini, cut into ¼-inch slices

2 red bell peppers

2 orange bell peppers

1 medium red onion, peeled and sliced

2 cups goat cheese

8 tablespoons pesto

Pinch of salt and pepper

Peachy Paleo Salsa (optional)

 ADD MEAT! Add 1 pound of skinless, boneless chicken breast. Grill for 5–6 minutes per side, or until the chicken cooked through. Remove from heat, dice and add to the quesadillas with the rest of the vegetables.

 MAKE IT VEGAN! Cut the goat cheese—this recipe has tons of flavor anyway.

 GO PALEO! Use Paleo Tortillas found in the "Substitutions" chapter.

 GLUTEN-FREE! Don't worry—the Paleo Tortillas found in the "Substitutions" chapter are gluten-free as well.

Corn Quesadillas

ACTIVE TIME: 30 MINUTES • TOTAL TIME: 40 MINUTES • SERVES 6

This recipe is a simple way to promote fresh ingredients—its result is a beautiful yet familiar dish.

2 ears corn, shucked

2 medium summer squash, halved lengthwise

½ small red onion, cut into ¼-inch-thick slices

1 red bell pepper, cut into ¼-inch-thick slices

1 jalapeno pepper

1 tablespoon fresh basil, torn

1 teaspoon fresh oregano, torn

1 clove garlic, minced

¼ teaspoon salt

¼ teaspoon cumin

6 flour tortillas

1 cup pepper jack cheese

1 tablespoon olive oil

1. Brush the vegetables with olive oil and preheat your grill to medium heat. Place the vegetables on the grill and cook until they become tender. They should take about 5–6 minutes per side. Remove from heat when the vegetables are tender.

2. Remove corn from cobs and dice the rest of the vegetables. Place these in a large bowl and mix in the basil, oregano, salt and cumin.

3. Evenly distribute the mixture between the 6 tortillas. Sprinkle cheese over the mixture and fold the tortillas over the filling.

4. Place the quesadillas on the grill for 1–2 minutes per side, or until they are heated through and the cheese has melted. Remove from heat, cut into wedges and serve.

 ADD MEAT! Add 1 pound of 1¼-inch-thick New York strip steak. Brush the steak on both sides with olive oil and season generously with salt and pepper. Grill on medium heat for 4–5 minutes, turn it over and cook for another 4–5 minutes for rare. Cook until the steak reaches desired tenderness, remove from heat and serve.

 MAKE IT VEGAN! Use a vegan cheese alternative from the "Substitutions" chapter.

 GO PALEO! Instead of brown rice, use the Cauliflower Rice. Additionally, remove the black beans and the cheese; get your protein by adding steak according to the directions in the "Add Meat" variation. Use Paleo Tortillas from the "Substitutions" section, or remove the wrap and make it a bowl.

 GLUTEN-FREE! Turn this into a burrito bowl! Simply remove the wrap and rice and add to a bowl!

Zucchini Veggie Burgers

ACTIVE TIME: 10 MINUTES • TOTAL TIME: 15 MINUTES • SERVES 4

This veggie burger is different from traditional veggie burgers because it uses zucchini as a main component. After discovering it, I'm surprised I don't encounter them more often.

1 cup black beans
1 cup zucchini, shredded
6 tablespoons flax seed, ground
½ teaspoon steak seasoning
4 hamburger buns

1. Rinse and drain the black beans.

2. Mix together all of the ingredients in a medium bowl, mashing them together with a fork. Let the mixture stand, then form 4 patties.

3. Preheat grill to medium-high heat. Grill the patties until they become golden on each side, about 4 minutes per. To prevent sticking, try brushing your grill with olive oil. Serve on a bun with your favorite condiments and toppings.

 ADD MEAT! Add a few strips of cooked bacon when topping the burgers.

 GO PALEO! Try chia seeds instead of the black beans. In this case, it may be easier to grill up a grass-fed beef burger instead.

 GLUTEN-FREE! Instead of using steak seasoning, try using a pinch of salt, pepper and dried thyme. Don't forget to serve on gluten-free buns.

Simple Veggie Quesadillas

ACTIVE TIME: 10 MINUTES • TOTAL TIME: 25 MINUTES • SERVES 4

These simple summer quesadillas are even better when using garden-fresh ingredients. They pack a delicious punch even though they're so easy to make!

1. Cut the zucchini and summer squash into ½-inch slices. Brush the vegetables with olive oil and salt.

2. Preheat grill to medium heat and cook the vegetables for 8–10 minutes, flipping halfway through. Cook until tender and remove from heat.

3. Chop your grilled veggies into bite-sized pieces and place them in a small bowl, mixing in chopped tomato.

4. Brush tortillas with olive oil and grill for about 2–3 minutes, at which point they should be golden brown.

5. Remove from heat and add in cheese and vegetables. Fold tortillas in half and grill for 2–3 more minutes, flipping halfway. Remove from heat when cheese is melted and serve.

1 medium zucchini, cut lengthwise
1 summer squash, cut lengthwise
2 bell peppers, cut in half lengthwise
1 medium roma tomato, chopped
2 tablespoons olive oil
½ teaspoon salt
5 ounces grated pepper jack cheese
4 whole wheat tortillas

 ADD MEAT! Add 1 pound of 1¼-inch thick New York strip steak. Brush the steak on both sides with olive oil and season generously with salt and pepper. Grill on medium heat for 4–5 minutes, turn over and cook for another 4–5 minutes for rare. Cook until the steak reaches desired tenderness. Remove from heat and dice.

 MAKE IT VEGAN! Don't add cheese when assembling the tacos, or use one of the options in the "Substitutions" section.

 GO PALEO! Remove or replace the cheese, and be sure to use the Paleo Tortillas in the "Substitutions" Section.

 GLUTEN-FREE! Use the Paleo Tortillas.

Thai Vegetable Tacos

ACTIVE TIME: 20 MINUTES • TOTAL TIME: 30 MINUTES • SERVES 6

Everybody loves Thai food, so why not make it in the backyard? This recipe is easy to adjust and provides a unique flavor you're unlikely to find in any restaurant.

1 medium eggplant

2 large tomatoes, cut in half

2 small zucchini

2 bell peppers (color is up to you)

¼ small red onion

6 white corn tortillas

1 medium avocado, sliced

¼ cup cilantro, minced

¼ cup olive oil

Thai Peanut Sauce ("Marinades & Sauces")

1. Slice eggplant, zucchini, bell peppers and onion into approximately ³/₄-inch-thick strips. Try to keep them approximately the same size so cooking times will stay similar.

2. Preheat your grill to medium-high heat. Brush the sliced vegetables with olive oil and place them on your grill. Cook until tender. For tomatoes, brush the cut side with olive oil and grill for about 4 minutes, or until grill marks appear. Make sure to flip the slices halfway through. Cooking times may vary, but eggplant and zucchini should take about 4–5 minutes per side, bell peppers about 2 minutes per side and onion about 3 minutes per side. Once they are all grilled to desired tenderness, remove from heat and slice into bite-sized cubes.

3. Make the peanut sauce by following the steps in the "Marinades & Sauces" chapter. In a large bowl, toss all of the grilled vegetables in 3 tablespoons of the sauce.

4. To heat the tortillas, place on the grill until they become slightly warm. Divide the vegetables evenly between the tortillas, add cilantro and sliced avocado and drizzle with the remaining peanut sauce.

ADD MEAT! Grill ½ pound of skinless, boneless chicken over medium heat for 5–6 minutes per side or until the chicken is fully cooked through. After removing the chicken from heat, dice and toss it in the peanut sauce before adding it to the tortillas.

 MAKE IT VEGAN! Make sure to make the peanut sauce using the vegan variation.

 GO PALEO! Use the paleo variation for your peanut sauce, and use the paleo tortillas found in the "Substitutions" section instead of flour tortillas.

 GLUTEN-FREE! Make sure to use paleo tortillas. Buy your own or use the Paleo Tortillas found in the "Substitutions" section instead of flour tortillas.

Vegetable Lettuce Wraps

ACTIVE TIME: 10 MINUTES • TOTAL TIME: 35 MINUTES • SERVES 4

Lettuce makes the perfect shell for this delicious filling.

2 tablespoons sesame oil

1 clove garlic, minced

⅛ tablespoon fresh ginger, minced

8 ounces shiitake mushroom caps, sliced

3 tablespoons soy sauce

2 bell peppers, sliced

1 cup asparagus, chopped

⅓ cup green onion, diced

½ cup brown rice

4 large pieces of romaine lettuce

Salt and pepper, to taste

1. Cook brown rice according to package instructions and set aside. Cut a piece of foil large enough to create a packet for the vegetables.

2. In a large bowl, mix together sesame oil, garlic, ginger, mushrooms and soy sauce. Add in bell peppers, asparagus and green onion. Toss to coat and transfer to foil. Fold the foil over and seal the packet by crimping the edges.

3. Preheat your grill to medium heat and place the packet seam side up on the grates. Cook for 10–15 minutes, remove and check for tenderness.

4. Once vegetables are properly cooked, return the mixture to the large bowl and mix in brown rice. Distribute the mixture to the pieces of lettuce and serve.

 ADD MEAT! Add 1 pound of meat (chicken, beef or whatever else you'd like!) and dice it into 1½-inch cubes. Toss with olive oil, add the cubes to the foil packets and cook until it has reached desired doneness. It may be easier to cook meat in a separate packet to ensure that it is fully cooked.

 GO PALEO! Instead of brown rice, use Cauliflower Rice from the "Substitutions" chapter. Additionally, use coconut aminos instead of soy sauce!

 GLUTEN-FREE! Instead of soy sauce, use coconut aminos or tamari to make this sauce gluten-free!

Grilled Asparagus Tacos

ACTIVE TIME: 10 MINUTES • TOTAL TIME: 15 MINUTES • SERVES 4

These simple tacos are just what you need when you want some delicious tacos in a pinch. They're easily developed, really tasty when paired with a corn salsa and the asparagus crunch plays nicely with a soft tortilla.

1. Preheat your grill to medium-high heat. Cook the asparagus spears until they soften and become slightly charred.

2. Remove the spears from heat once tender and evenly spread them between the tortillas. Add salsa, cheese, salt and pepper and serve.

1 bunch asparagus spears

4 tortillas

Corn Salsa ("Sides & Salads")

⅓ cup shredded cheddar cheese

Pinch of salt and pepper

 ADD MEAT! Add seasoned, cooked ground beef to the tacos for some extra flavor and protein.

 MAKE IT VEGAN! Remove the cheese and replace with Moxarella from "Substitutions."

 GO PALEO! Replace corn tortillas with paleo tortillas, or turn the tacos into a salad. Remove the cheddar cheese and replace with a paleo cheese of your choosing from "Substitutions."

 GLUTEN-FREE! Using paleo tortillas or turning this into a salad is a delicious option.

Avocado Tacos

**ACTIVE TIME: 15–20 MINUTES • TOTAL TIME: 35 MINUTES •
SERVING SIZE: 6 TO 8 TACOS**

These avocado tacos are light, refreshing and easy to make on a hot summer day.

FILLING

1 small zucchini, diced

1 small summer squash (diced)

½ medium red onion (diced)

1 ear of sweet corn
(removed from cob)

1 cup of cherry tomatoes (sliced)

2 tablespoons olive oil

2 cloves garlic (minced)

2 teaspoons cumin

¼ teaspoon salt

Tortillas

Shredded cheese of your choosing

2 Serrano peppers, coarsely
chopped (optional)

AVOCADO CREMA

1 ripe avocado

⅓ cup plain Greek yogurt

¼ cup cilantro, minced

1 tablespoon lime juice

1. Prepare large pieces of heavy-duty foil—6 pieces should be enough. Preheat your grill to medium-high heat. Toss your chopped vegetables with olive oil, garlic, salt and cumin.

2. Evenly divide the vegetables among the pieces of foil. Fold edges of foil and crimp to create a sealed packet. Place the packets on the grill, seal side up. Roast the vegetables until they become tender and slightly brown. This process should take about 20–25 minutes. Open one packet and taste to make sure the vegetables are tender and crisp before removing from heat.

3. While the vegetables are roasting, create your avocado crema by processing the avocado crema ingredients together in a food processor or blender. Process until mixture reaches desired thickness.

4. Assemble tacos by warming up tortillas and adding the roasted veggies, avocado crema, cheese and some cilantro. For an extra burst of heat, serve alongside chopped Serrano pepper.

 ADD MEAT!   Add 1 pound of boneless chicken to the grill. This should take about 5 to 6 minutes per side. When the meat is fully cooked, remove, dice and add to tacos.

 MAKE IT VEGAN!   Substitute plain Greek yogurt with ¼ cup canned full fat coconut milk when making your avocado crema.

 GO PALEO!   Substitute your taco shells with Paleo Tortillas ("Substitutions") or create a taco salad instead.

 GLUTEN-FREE!   Use Paleo Tortillas.

Black Bean Quesadillas

ACTIVE TIME: 10 MINUTES • TOTAL TIME: 15 MINUTES • SERVES 4

The marriage of black beans, fresh tomatoes and bell peppers give this quesadilla the right balance of vitamins and protein.

1. In a large bowl, toss together black beans, tomatoes, bell peppers, cheese, cilantro, red pepper flakes and onion. Mix evenly.

2. Assemble quesadillas by laying out tortillas and dividing the mixture evenly over 4 of them. Place the remaining tortillas on top.

3. Preheat grill to medium heat and brush oil on the grates. Place the quesadillas on the grates and cook until cheese has melted, flipping the quesadillas halfway through. It should take about 2 minutes per side. Remove from heat and serve.

1 (15-ounce) can black beans, rinsed and drained
2 medium tomatoes, diced
2 bell peppers, sliced
10 ounces cheddar cheese, grated
1 teaspoon cups cilantro, chopped
1 teaspoon red pepper flakes
½ cup white onion, chopped
8 large flour tortillas
1 tablespoon vegetable oil
Salt and pepper, to taste

 ADD MEAT! Grill up some flank steak. Grill over medium heat for about 6 minutes, or until it reaches desired tenderness. Remove from heat, slice, and add to the quesadillas.

 MAKE IT VEGAN! Replace the cheese with vegan cheddar cheese, or one of the alternatives in the "Substitutions" section. The vegan cheddar can be found at most supermarkets.

 GO PALEO! Replace the black beans with 1 pound of grass-fed flank steak, as described in the "Add Meat" variation. Slice and add to the quesadillas. Make sure to use Paleo Tortillas and remove the cheese.

 GLUTEN-FREE! Use the Paleo Tortillas.

Couscous and Grilled Veggies

ACTIVE TIME: 10 MINUTES • TOTAL TIME: 25 MINUTES • SERVES 5

There are many ways to make this dish, but I prefer the Dijon flavor. Be sure to mix in the olive oil slowly so your mixture emulsifies properly.

3 ears corn, shucked

3 medium zucchini

5 medium tomatoes

2 cups cooked couscous

1 (15-ounce) can garbanzo beans, rinsed and drained

6 basil leaves, torn

2 tablespoons olive oil

1 tablespoon Dijon mustard

¼ cup olive oil

⅛ cup balsamic vinegar

⅛ cup red wine vinegar

1. Prepare the vegetables by cutting the zucchini into thick rounds and the tomatoes into bite-sized chunks.

2. Cook couscous according to package instructions and let stand.

3. Preheat your grill to medium-high heat. Brush the corn and zucchini with olive oil until they are evenly coated. Place them on the grill and cook until grill marks appear, making sure to rotate the corn and zucchini occasionally. This should take about 8 minutes.

4. Once the vegetables are as tender as you like, remove from heat and cut the kernels off the cob. In a large bowl, toss together corn, zucchini, tomatoes, couscous, garbanzo beans and basil.

5. In a small bowl, mix together Dijon mustard, olive oil, balsamic vinegar, and red wine vinegar. Pour into the large bowl, toss and serve.

 ADD MEAT! Serve this with 1 pound of skinless, boneless chicken breast grilled over medium heat for 5–6 minutes on each side.

 GO PALEO! Replace couscous with Cauliflower Rice. Remove the beans and serve the veggies with lamb chops. For the lamb chops, combine 1 minced shallot, 1 teaspoon of dried oregano, 1 teaspoon of black pepper, 1 teaspoon of salt, ¼ cup of olive oil, 3 cloves of minced garlic and 2 tablespoons of lemon juice in a small bowl. Mix well and pour the marinade over 6 lamb chops in a large bag. Marinate in the refrigerator for at least 1 hour and then grill on high heat until tender, about 5 minutes per side.

 GLUTEN-FREE! Replace couscous with white rice.

Corn and Zucchini Burgers

ACTIVE TIME: 10 MINUTES • TOTAL TIME: 30 MINUTES • SERVES 4

There's more than one way to make a zucchini burger. This one utilizes corn and chickpeas for a more diverse flavor.

6 cups zucchini, shredded

2 cups chickpeas

¼ cup green onions, chopped

1 cup corn kernels

4 cups flaky bread crumbs

2 teaspoons baking powder

1 teaspoon baking soda

2 teaspoons salt

1 teaspoon red pepper flakes

2 cups drained zucchini juice

Pepper, to taste

1 tablespoon olive oil

4 hamburger buns

1. Shred and drain your zucchini into a small bowl. Drain by squeezing out all of the water until it's dry. Collect the liquid and set aside.

2. In a food processor, add chickpeas, onions, corn, breadcrumbs, baking powder, baking soda, salt, red pepper flakes and a pinch of pepper. Process the dry ingredients and add the zucchini juice slowly until the ingredients have become smooth. Transfer to a large bowl.

3. Mix in the veggies and create patties by separating the mixture into 4 even parts. Pack the mixture into a ¼ measuring cup and then turn it into a flattened patty.

4. Preheat grill to medium heat. Brush patties with olive oil and place them on the grill. Cook until each side is golden brown, which should take about 15 minutes. Be sure to flip halfway! Remove from heat and serve on a bun or lettuce leaf.

 ADD MEAT! Grill up slices of bacon or ham and add to the toppings of the burger, or even the patty mix.

 GO PALEO! Since chickpeas and breadcrumbs are not paleo, grill up a grass-fed beef burger instead. It will save you the trouble of trying to produce this burger without the main ingredient!

 GLUTEN-FREE! This burger is very difficult to produce without gluten, instead grill up a regular beef burger and serve it on a gluten-free bun.

Mushroom Veggie Burgers

ACTIVE TIME: 15 MINUTES • TOTAL TIME: 25 MINUTES • SERVES 6

A classic. As you may know by now, veggie burgers are a tough egg to crack. They often fall apart without the consistency of a regular beef burger, making them difficult to love. Fear not: This burger hasn't failed me yet and tastes delicious.

1. Simmer 1½ cups of water and add the cups amaranth. This should take 25 minutes and can be done at any time before making the patties.

2. Finely chop the mushrooms and the spinach. In a medium bowl, mix together the cooked amaranth, mushrooms, spinach, carrot, flour and ground flax. Add a pinch of salt and pepper. Mix well and let it sit.

3. Preheat your grill to medium-high heat and oil the grates. Once the mixture has sat, make 6 patties and place them on the grill. Cook each side until they become golden, which should take about 4–5 minutes per side. Serve on buns with your favorite condiments.

1½ cups cooked amaranth
3 ounces baby portobello mushrooms
1 cup spinach
1 large carrot, shredded
½ cup oat flour
¼ cup ground flax
Salt and pepper, to taste
¼ cup olive oil

 ADD MEAT! Cook up a few slices of ham and toss them on top of the burger for some extra flavor.

 GO PALEO! Since amaranth is a grain, it's off the paleo menu. You would be better off grilling up a grass-fed beef burger instead.

 GLUTEN-FREE! Make sure to buy gluten-free buns.

Quinoa Burger

Veggie burgers with a quinoa base are harder to come by, but no less delicious. Don't skimp on the spices, as the quinoa absorbs them beautifully.

1½ cup quinoa

2 cups vegetable stock

½ cup tomato sauce

1 tablespoon tomato paste

2 kale leaves, finely chopped

1 tablespoon thyme, chopped

1 tablespoon oregano, chopped

1 cup shiitake mushrooms, finely chopped

2 tablespoons olive oil

Salt and pepper, to taste

1. In a pot, add quinoa, vegetable stock, tomato sauce, kale, thyme and oregano. Heat on high until the mixture begins to boil. Cover, reduce heat to low and let simmer until the liquid is absorbed. This should take about 20 minutes.

2. Remove from heat and add tomato paste and mushrooms. Add as much salt and pepper as you like, then let the mixture cool.

3. Preheat your grill to medium heat. Once cool, separate the mixture into about 5–6 patties. Grill for a few minutes on each side or until the patties are completely heated through. Serve on a bun or lettuce leaf.

 ADD MEAT! Grill up slices of bacon or ham and top your burger off.

 GO PALEO! Since quinoa isn't paleo, I suggest you grill up a grass-fed beef burger instead. It will save you the trouble of trying to produce this burger without the main ingredient.

Spicy Grilled Cheese

ACTIVE TIME: 5 MINUTES • TOTAL TIME: 5 MINUTES • SERVES 1 SANDWICH

This is definitely the perfect meal if you want to make sure everybody gets what they want—who doesn't love grilled cheese? By using rich, flavorful bread and some more unique ingredients, create the fun twist on a classic lunch.

2 slices fresh bread
(ex: sourdough, rye, Italian)

2 jalapeno peppers, cut in half

3 ounces cheddar cheese, shredded

1 tablespoon melted butter

1 tablespoon olive oil

1. Preheat your grill to medium-low heat. Keep in mind that grilling with the lid down will allow the cheese to melt and cook the bread more evenly. Coat sliced jalapenos in olive oil with a pinch of salt and pepper. Place directly on the grill and cook for 5 to 10 minutes, or until skin has charred. Remove from heat.

2. Distribute the cheese evenly over a slice of bread. Place grilled jalapenos on top of cheese and add the second layer of bread.

3. Brush a layer of melted butter on the top piece of bread. Lay the sandwich on the grill buttered side down, pressing down on it lightly. Close the lid and let cook for about 2 minutes. Once the bread has reached desired crispness, flip and repeat. Remove from heat, slice and serve.

 ADD MEAT! Add four thin slices of cooked ham when adding the cheese. It should crisp up perfectly on the grill.

 MAKE IT VEGAN! Use the Moxarella recipe from "Substitutions."

 GO PALEO! Find paleo bread at your local supermarket.

 GLUTEN-FREE! Find gluten-free bread at your local supermarket.

Vegan Grilled Cheese

ACTIVE TIME: 15 MINUTES • TOTAL TIME: 25 MINUTES • SERVES 4

This simple grilled cheese utilizes beans and vegan mozzarella cheese! It may not taste like a traditional grilled cheese, but after trying it, you won't want it to.

1. Rinse and drain the black beans and set them aside.

2. Slice the peppers and brush them with olive oil. Grill over medium heat for 5–6 minutes per side, or until pepper strips become tender.

3. Remove from heat, dice and place in a medium bowl. Mix with the beans and distribute over 4 slices of bread.

4. Distribute Moxarella between the sandwiches and top with remaining slices of bread.

5. Place on the grill and grill the sandwiches until the bread becomes golden brown. Remove from heat and serve!

8 slices bread
Moxarella ("Substitutions")
1 bell pepper, sliced
1 (15-ounce) can black beans
1 tablespoon olive oil

 ADD MEAT!   Add slices of cooked bacon to the sandwich!

 MAKE IT VEGAN!   This recipe is already vegan! You can buy your own vegan mozzarella, or use the Moxarella recipe in the "Substitutions" chapter.

 GO PALEO!   Use paleo bread.

 GLUTEN-FREE!   Use gluten-free bread.

Black Bean Burger

A delicious veggie burger that's sure to have even the most dedicated carnivore salivating.

1. Begin by rinsing the beans and completely drying them. Once they are completely dry, add them to a medium bowl and mash them until they become thick and pasty.

2. Using a food processor, finely chop the red bell pepper, onion and garlic. Before adding the beans, be sure to strain the vegetables and remove excess water—this will help keep the burgers together. If you don't remove all excess water, your burger will come apart in a mushy heap.

3. Preheat your grill to high heat. In a small bowl, mix together the egg, cumin, chili powder and any additional hot sauce you'd like to add. Add this to the bean and vegetable mixture and stir in bread crumbs until the mixture sticks together and holds well.

4. Separate the mixture into four patties. Grill for about 8 minutes on each side, remove from heat and serve on a bun with condiments of your choosing.

1 (16 ounces) can black beans
½ red bell pepper, cut into strips
½ small red onion, sliced
2 cloves garlic, peeled
2 eggs
1 teaspoon cumin
1 tablespoon chili powder
1 cup bread crumbs

 ADD MEAT! Cook up strips of bacon to serve on the burger.

 MAKE IT VEGAN! ¹/₂ cup of avocado is a good substitute for the 2 eggs in this recipe.

 GO PALEO! Because most beans aren't considered paleo, grill up a grass-fed beef burger.

 GLUTEN-FREE! Substitute bread crumbs with rolled oats.

Grilled Veggie Paninis

ACTIVE TIME: 10 MINUTES • TOTAL TIME: 20 MINUTES • SERVES 4

These paninis are incredibly delicious and can be made in no time. Make these with the bread you like the most and press down with a spatula to really add in those grill marks.

1 medium zucchini

1 medium summer squash

1 medium onion

2 medium portobello mushrooms

1 cup mozzarella cheese

8 slices Italian bread

Olive oil

Pinch of salt and pepper

1. Preheat grill to medium-high heat. Cut zucchini, squash and onion into ½-inch slices. Brush these slices with olive oil and sprinkle salt and pepper over oiled slices.

2. Begin grilling onions first, cooking for 2–3 minutes, then add the rest of the veggies. Cook for 6–8 minutes and turn occasionally. Cook until vegetables become tender and remove.

3. Brush bread with oil. Grill for 1–2 minutes, turn over and sprinkle cheese. When the cheese is slightly melted, add the sliced portobello mushrooms, zucchini, squash and onion.

4. Grill the sandwich on both sides until slight grill marks appear. Slice and serve.

 ADD MEAT! Add a few slices of ham or turkey to each panini before grilling.

 MAKE IT VEGAN! Replace mozzarella cheese with Moxarella from "Substitutions."

 GO PALEO! Find almond-based, paleo-friendly bread at your local supermarket and use that instead of Italian bread. Remove the cheese from the recipe ore use a replacement from the "Substitutions" section.

 GLUTEN-FREE! Use gluten-free bread instead of Italian bread. This can be found at most supermarkets.

Roasted Eggplant Sandwich

ACTIVE TIME: 15 MINUTES • TOTAL TIME: 25 MINUTES • SERVES 2

This is one of my favorite lunches, and it's just as delicious without the bread.

1. In a small bowl, mix soy sauce, lemon juice and garlic together. Brush this mixture on both sides of the eggplant and preheat your grill to medium heat.

2. Grill the slices for 5–8 minutes per side, or until they become tender and brown. Grill the onion slices the same way, cooking until tender.

3. Lightly toast the bread on the grill and assemble the sandwiches by spreading mayo on each slice and piling them with grilled eggplant, onions and some arugula.

1 medium eggplant, cut into ½-inch rounds

3 tablespoons soy sauce

1 tablespoon lemon juice

1 clove garlic, minced

1 small red onion, thinly sliced

1 handful of fresh arugula

2 tablespoons Paleo Mayonnaise ("Substitutions")

4 slices of bread

 ADD MEAT! Cook up a few strips of bacon for each sandwich.

 GO PALEO! Replace soy sauce with coconut aminos and use paleo bread.

 GLUTEN-FREE! Replace soy sauce with coconut aminos or tamari and use gluten-free bread.

Grilled Black Bean Burrito

ACTIVE TIME: 20 MINUTES • TOTAL TIME: 30 MINUTES • SERVING SIZE: 6

Making you feel like you have a Chipotle in your own backyard, this protein-packed burrito comes with all the fixings.

1 cup brown rice

1 can (16 ounces) black beans

1 large yellow squash,
cut into long slices

1 large zucchini, cut into
long slices

2 ears corn, shucked

1 small red onion, chopped

¼ cup chopped cilantro

1 tablespoon olive oil

6 large flour tortillas

2 tomatoes, diced

1 cup pepper jack cheese, grated

Pinch of salt

Peachy Paleo Salsa (optional)

1. Begin by cooking the rice, using the package instructions specific to the rice you're using. Once it has cooked completely, mix in the cilantro and let sit.

2. Preheat your grill to medium-high heat. Brush squash, zucchini and corn with olive oil. Grill until tender, making sure that veggies do not become too soft. Be sure to turn them during cooking. This should take about 10 minutes. Remove from heat and dice.

3. While the vegetables are grilling, rinse the black beans. You can heat them in a saucepan or just eat them as is. Additionally, chop the onion and tomato.

4. Once everything is prepared, begin assembling your burritos! On the flour tortillas, layer rice, beans, veggies, onions, tomatoes and cheese. Wrap them up tightly and place on the grill for about 1 minute per side. Remove from heat and serve. If you're so inclined, whip up some Peachy Paleo Salsa and drizzle on top of the burrito!

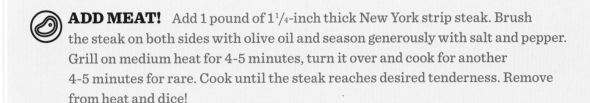 **ADD MEAT!**   Add 1 pound of 1¼-inch thick New York strip steak. Brush the steak on both sides with olive oil and season generously with salt and pepper. Grill on medium heat for 4-5 minutes, turn it over and cook for another 4-5 minutes for rare. Cook until the steak reaches desired tenderness. Remove from heat and dice!

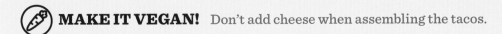 **MAKE IT VEGAN!**   Don't add cheese when assembling the tacos.

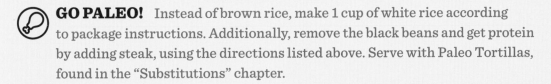 **GO PALEO!**   Instead of brown rice, make 1 cup of white rice according to package instructions. Additionally, remove the black beans and get protein by adding steak, using the directions listed above. Serve with Paleo Tortillas, found in the "Substitutions" chapter.

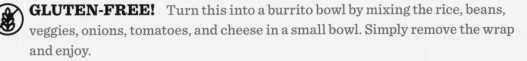 **GLUTEN-FREE!**   Turn this into a burrito bowl by mixing the rice, beans, veggies, onions, tomatoes, and cheese in a small bowl. Simply remove the wrap and enjoy.

Cauliflower Steaks

ACTIVE TIME: 15 MINUTES • TOTAL TIME: 30 MINUTES • SERVES 4

Steak isn't just for meat-eaters. Try this gluten-free option using cauliflower from the garden, pair with some red wine and enjoy.

1 large cauliflower

¼ cup olive oil

1 tablespoon lemon juice

2 cloves garlic, minced

Shredded pepper jack cheese

1 pinch red pepper flakes, to taste

Salt and pepper, to taste

1. Begin by slicing the cauliflower lengthwise through the core into four pieces—these will become your "steaks." Preheat your grill to medium-high heat.

2. Mix the olive oil, lemon juice, garlic, pepper flakes, salt and pepper with a whisk.

3. Place the steaks into foil large enough to surround the steaks and seal them into a packet. Generously brush the mixture on both sides of the cauliflower. Seal the packet and place on the grill. Cook for about 8 minutes, or until tender. Flip the steaks about halfway through.

4. Once it is slightly browned, remove from heat, sprinkle shredded pepper jack over the tops and serve.

 ADD MEAT! Grill up some grass-fed flank steak. Prep the steak for grilling. Marinate the steak with one of the marinades from the "Substitutions" section, up to 12 hours prior to grilling, and for at least 4 hours. Grill each side for about 6 minutes (rare), or until desired tenderness. Dice and serve with the cauliflower.

 MAKE IT VEGAN! This recipe tastes just as good without the cheese! Remove the cheese to make this completely vegan.

 GO PALEO! Remove the cheese and eat these cauliflower steaks with steak! Grill up some grass-fed flank steak following the directions in the "Add Meat" step.

BBQ and Lemon Tofu

ACTIVE TIME: 20 MINUTES • TOTAL TIME: 35 MINUTES • SERVES 3

Making great tofu is the perfect way for vegetarians to enjoy a barbecue. This marinade soaks beautifully into your large tofu chunks.

1. Slice the tofu into ½-inch-thick slices. Drain by placing tofu between paper towels and pressing out remaining liquids, or by placing a weight on top and letting the tofu drain for about 30 minutes. Once the pieces are properly drained, cut them into ½-inch cubes.

2. Mix the rest of the ingredients well in a large plastic bag. Add the tofu cubes and marinate in the refrigerator for at least two hours.

3. Preheat the grill to medium-high heat and thread the cubes onto skewers for easier grilling. Lightly oil the surface of the grill and cook the cubes for about 10 to 15 minutes, or until the tofu becomes slightly browned. Remove from skewers and serve with sliced vegetables!

1 pound firm tofu
½ cup olive oil
⅓ cup lemon juice
2 teaspoons dried oregano
1 teaspoon Dijon mustard
½ teaspoon garlic salt
2 teaspoons ground cumin

 ADD MEAT! Slice 1 pound of boneless, skinless chicken into cubes. Marinate instead of the tofu and grill until the meat is no longer pink. Serve with vegetables.

 MAKE IT VEGAN! This recipe is already vegan, but for more flavor and nutrition add some peppers and zucchini to the skewers.

 GO PALEO! Unfortunately, tofu doesn't qualify as paleo since it's made from processed soybeans. To add some protein to this meal, simply use the chicken directions in the "Add Meat" section.

 GLUTEN-FREE! Most Dijon mustard is not gluten-free, so be sure to purchase organic, gluten-free Dijon mustard for the marinade! Additionally, make sure you purchase unflavored tofu to ensure that it is gluten-free.

Basmati Rice Stuffed Peppers

ACTIVE TIME: 15 MINUTES • TOTAL TIME: 50 MINUTES • SERVES 4

I love stuffed peppers; I love stuffed peppers even more when they're on the grill. You'll find this to be an easy recipe despite slightly longer wait time.

RICE

1½ cups brown basmati rice
1 large tomato
1 large carrot
1 small summer squash
1 medium zucchini
½ large yellow or white onion
1 tablespoon olive oil
2 teaspoons oregano
1 teaspoon thyme
2 cups water
1 tablespoon red wine vinegar
3 cloves garlic
2 tablespoons lemon juice
Salt and pepper, to taste

BEANS

1 (15-ounce) can white beans
2 tablespoons red wine vinegar
1 tablespoon olive oil
4 large bell peppers, any color

1. Rinse the basmati rice through a strainer and let it sit.

2. Puree the large tomato using a food processor until it turns into juice. Chop onion, carrot, summer squash and zucchini into dime-sized slices. Save 2 tablespoon of the chopped onion and set it aside for the beans.

3. In a large pot, heat olive oil over medium heat and add onion until it starts to brown. Add the carrot, summer squash, zucchini, oregano and thyme, letting this cook for about 1 minute. Add in the rice, pureed tomato and water, plus a pinch of salt, and bring the mixture to a boil. Cover the pot when it reaches a boil and reduce heat to low, so that the mixture is simmering. Cook until all of the water is absorbed and rice is completely cooked. This should take about 35 minutes.

4. While this is cooking, place beans, the extra 2 tablespoons of onions, olive oil, red wine vinegar and oregano into the food processor. Let this run until the mixture becomes smooth. Once the rice has finished cooking, mix in the garlic, red wine vinegar and lemon juice. Cover again and let stand for about 1 minute. Season with salt and pepper to your preferred taste.

5. To prepare the bell peppers, cut them in half lengthwise and scrape out the seeds. Discard the seeds and distribute the bean mixture evenly between the 8 halves. Be sure to spread the mixture along the bottom so as to leave room for the rice. Next, distribute the rice mixture as well.

6. Preheat grill to medium-low heat and oil the grates. Lightly brush oil onto the peppers to prevent sticking. Place the stuffed peppers on the grill and cook for about 10–12 minutes. Once they begin to show slight grill marks, remove from heat and serve.

 ADD MEAT! Add ½ pound of cooked ground beef to the mixture, mixing it in with the veggies!

 GO PALEO! Replace brown rice with Cauliflower Rice from "Substitutions," or white rice if you count it as a "safe starch." Additionally, make the mixture without the beans as they aren't part of a paleo diet.

 GLUTEN-FREE! Replace brown rice with white rice!

Grilled Eggplant and Spinach

ACTIVE TIME: 10 MINUTES • TOTAL TIME: 15 MINUTES • SERVES 4

This tasty standard is packed with nutrients. Play with the barbecue rub to get the exact flavor you want—the eggplant serves as a great vessel for whatever you decide.

2 small eggplants, cut into ½-inch slices

Barbecue Rub

2 cups baby spinach

1 cup brown rice

1. Cook brown rice according to package instructions and let stand.

2. In a small bowl, make the barbecue rub from the "Marinades" section—this should only take a minute. Brush this mixture over both sides of the eggplant and let them sit for at least 5 minutes.

3. Preheat your grill to medium heat and cook the slices until they become tender. This should take about 4–5 minutes per side. Remove from heat and serve over rice with spinach.

 ADD MEAT! Serve this with 1 pound of skinless, boneless chicken breast. Grill over medium heat for 5–6 minutes, or until thoroughly cooked through.

 GO PALEO! Remove the rice and serve over Paleo Pork Chops, using the recipe in the "Substitutions" chapter.

 GLUTEN FREE! Replace the brown rice with white rice.

Summer Squash Sandwiches

ACTIVE TIME: 10 MINUTES • TOTAL TIME: 25 MINUTES • SERVES 4

Sandwiches make a great lunch or dinner! I get sick of eating the same boring sandwiches, so I like to make mine with fresh summer squash and garden ripe tomatoes.

1. Preheat your grill to medium heat. Slice your summer squash into ¼-inch-thick rounds. In a large bowl, mix olive oil, balsamic vinegar and red wine vinegar. Add the squash slices to the bowl and toss to coat.

2. Arrange half of the slices on a tray and top each with a tomato slice, crumbled feta and torn bits of basil. After adding salt and pepper, top with the remaining squash slices.

3. Lightly oil your grill to prevent sticking. Place the mini sandwiches on the grill and cook for about 6 minutes, or until grill marks appear and the bottom slice is tender. Carefully flip your sandwiches and cook for another 6 minutes, or until they've reached desired tenderness. Remove from heat and serve.

1 medium summer squash
3 medium tomatoes, sliced
11 ounces feta cheese
4 tablespoons olive oil
1 tablespoon balsamic vinegar
1 tablespoon red wine vinegar
Salt and pepper, to taste
Fresh basil leaves, torn

 ADD MEAT! Serve with grilled chicken. Cook ½ pound of skinless, boneless chicken breast on medium heat for 5–6 minutes, or until it reaches desired doneness.

 MAKE IT VEGAN! Replace the cheese with one of the vegan substitutes.

 GO PALEO! Remove cheese from the recipe and use paleo bread. You could also turn this into a wrap by using the Paleo Tortilla recipe in the "Substitutions" section.

 GLUTEN-FREE! Use gluten-free bread.

MLT: Mushroom, Lettuce and Tomato

ACTIVE TIME: 5 MINUTES • TOTAL TIME: 20 MINUTES • SERVES 4

Who needs bacon when you have mushrooms? You can also make this with any veggie you prefer, or perhaps even beets to make it a true BLT.

4 large portobello mushrooms

2 tablespoons olive oil

1 teaspoon garlic seasoning

2 tablespoons mayonnaise

2 cups mixed greens

1 medium tomato, slices

8 slices of whole wheat bread

1. Preheat grill to medium heat. Brush your mushrooms with olive oil and sprinkle with garlic seasoning. Place them on the grill and cook for about 15–18 minutes, turning halfway through. Remove from heat when they turn golden brown and cut them into thin slices.

2. Toast bread on the grill for about 1 minute per side. Assemble your MLT by lightly spreading mayo on the toast and topping with salad greens, tomato slices and mushrooms. Serve and enjoy.

 ADD MEAT! To make it a real BLT, cook up as many strips of bacon as you would like and add them to the sandwich.

 MAKE IT VEGAN! Replace mayonnaise with vegan mayo, found in most supermarkets.

 GO PALEO! Use the Paleo Mayo recipe in the "Substitutions" section. Make sure to use paleo bread as well.

 GLUTEN-FREE! Replace the whole wheat bread with gluten-free bread!

Eggs on the Grill

While this is one of the few recipes that cannot be adjusted to fit a vegan diet, it's still one of my favorite things to make due to how simple it is. This meal is perfect for camping, or any casual setting really.

1. Preheat your grill to medium-high heat. Use a disposable foil pan, or any muffin pan, and coat the holes with olive oil. Crack an egg into each hole and add a few pieces of bell pepper.

2. Place this on the grill and cook for about 2 minutes, or until eggs reach desired doneness.

Disposable foil muffin pans

12 eggs

1 bell pepper, diced

 ADD MEAT!   Add a piece of crumbled, cooked bacon or ham over each egg.

 MAKE IT VEGAN!   Unfortunately, this recipe cannot be made vegan.

Pita Pizzas

Personal pies with a twist, this is a fun dish to make with a group so as to mix and match toppings.

1 cup grape tomatoes, halved

2 bell peppers, sliced

1 small red onion, sliced

⅓ cup fresh parsley

2 tablespoons olive oil

¾ cup hummus

4 whole pita breads

4 ounces feta, crumbled

1. In a small bowl, toss tomatoes, bell peppers, onions, parsley and olive oil.

2. Spread hummus over your pitas and top with the tomato mixture. Sprinkle crumbled feta over the pitas and preheat your grill to medium heat.

3. Place the pizzas on the grill and cook for 4–5 minutes, or until the bottoms are slightly charred and golden brown. Remove from heat and serve.

 ADD MEAT! Add slices of torn cooked ham to the top of the pita breads before cooking. They should crisp up nicely on the grill.

 MAKE IT VEGAN! Remove cheese from the recipe and top with 1 diced bell pepper instead. Feel free to use vegan shredded cheese as well.

 GO PALEO! Use the Paleo Pizza Dough recipe from "Substitutions."

 GLUTEN-FREE! Use the Gluten-Free Pizza Dough recipe from "Substitutions."

Spicy Chickpea Fajitas

ACTIVE TIME: 15 MINUTES • TOTAL TIME: 25 MINUTES • SERVES 4

This delicious alternative to tacos makes the perfect meal any night of the week. They take no time to make and have a nice kick to them that you'll keep thinking about long after you finish eating. As always, the chickpeas are easily replaced by meat or veggies.

1. Cut a piece of foil large enough to hold the chickpeas, tomatoes and onion and create a foil packet. Season with olive oil and paprika.

2. Cook this packet on the grill over medium heat for 15–20 minutes, or until the chickpeas become lightly browned. Remove from heat and set aside.

3. In a small bowl, mash the avocado and mix in the lime juice.

4. Char tortillas slightly on the grill and top them with chickpeas, tomatoes, onions and avocado. Wrap them up and serve.

1 (15-ounce) can chickpeas
1 tablespoon olive oil
¼ teaspoon paprika
2 tomatoes, sliced
1 small red onion, diced
1 avocado, peeled and sliced
1 tablespoon lime juice
4 tortillas

 ADD MEAT! Instead of the chickpeas, cook up 1 pound of skinless, boneless chicken breast. Slice it into cubes and cook it just like you'd cook the chickpeas. Be sure to grill the chicken until it is completely cooked through.

 GO PALEO! Remove the chickpeas and cook up chicken breast just like in the meat variation! Don't forget to serve with Paleo Tortillas ("Substitutions").

 GLUTEN-FREE! Serve with Paleo Tortillas.

Grilled Corn and Beans over Quinoa

ACTIVE TIME: 10 MINUTES • TOTAL TIME: 25 MINUTES • SERVES 4

Enjoy a full and balanced meal in the time it takes to go pick up a frozen pizza.

1 teaspoon vegetable oil

1 onion, chopped

3 cloves garlic, chopped

¾ cup quinoa

1½ cups vegetable broth

1 teaspoon cumin

¼ teaspoon cayenne pepper

2 ears corn, shucked

1 teaspoon olive oil

1 (15-ounce) can black beans

1 (15-ounce) can kidney beans

1 avocado, halved, pitted and chopped

½ cup fresh cilantro, chopped

1. Heat vegetable oil in a saucepan over medium heat. Add chopped onion and garlic and cook until they become lightly browned. Add the quinoa and vegetable broth to the mixture and bring it to a boil. Season the mixture with cumin, cayenne pepper and a pinch of salt and pepper. Once it reaches a boil, cover and reduce heat. Let it simmer for about 20 minutes, or until the quinoa becomes tender.

2. While your quinoa and vegetables simmer, preheat your grill to medium-high heat. Brush the corn with olive oil and place the two ears of corn directly on the grill. Grill for about 8 minutes, turning the corn regularly until it becomes lightly charred. Let it cool for a bit, and then cut the kernels off the cob and into the saucepan.

3. Remove from heat and mix in black beans, white beans, avocado, and cilantro. Serve and enjoy.

 ADD MEAT!   Add 1 pound of boneless chicken to the grill. Grilling should take about 5 to 6 minutes per side. When fully cooked, remove, dice and add to the salad!

 GO PALEO!   Assemble this dish without the quinoa or beans. Serve it over 1 or 2 cups of fresh baby spinach leaves or over grass-fed beef! Prepare ½ pound of steak for grilling by brushing with olive oil and sprinkling with salt and pepper. Grill each side for about 6 minutes (rare) over medium heat, or until desired tenderness. Dice and add to the salad.

Cajun Grilled Eggplant

ACTIVE TIME: 10 MINUTES • TOTAL TIME: 20 MINUTES • SERVES 5

This is a versatile recipe that goes really well served over rice, pasta or with any grilled meat. You can never go wrong making something Cajun-style.

1 cup brown rice

2 small eggplants, cut into ½-inch slices

¼ cup olive oil

2 tablespoons lime juice

1 tablespoon Cajun seasoning

1. Cook brown rice according to package instructions and let stand.

2. In a small bowl, mix together olive oil, lime juice and Cajun seasoning. Brush this mixture over both sides of the eggplant and let them sit for about 5 minutes.

3. Preheat your grill to medium heat and cook the slices until they become tender. This should take about 4–5 minutes per side. Remove from heat and serve over rice.

 ADD MEAT! Serve this with 1 pound of skinless, boneless chicken breast. Grill over medium heat for 5–6 minutes, until thoroughly cooked through.

 GO PALEO! Remove the rice and serve over Paleo Pork Chops, found in the "Substitutions" section.

 GLUTEN-FREE! Replace the brown rice with white rice.

Basil Grilled Cheese

ACTIVE TIME: 10 MINUTES • TOTAL TIME: 20 MINUTES • SERVES 4

With its focus on basil and mozzarella, this grilled cheese has a bit of Italian flare. It tastes especially delicious when made on a grill. Switch out the bread to make it your own!

1. Layer the cheese and tomato slices on 4 slices of bread. Sprinkle basil, balsamic and red wine vinegar, salt and pepper over the top. Add the top slice of bread.

2. In a small bowl, mix together oil and minced garlic. Brush over the outside of each slice of bread.

3. Preheat grill to medium heat, place sandwiches on grill and toast both sides until they are golden brown and the cheese has melted. Serve and enjoy.

8 slices whole wheat bread
8 slices mozzarella cheese
2 large plum tomatoes, sliced
12 fresh basil leaves, torn
1 teaspoon balsamic vinegar
1 teaspoon red wine vinegar
Salt and pepper, to taste
¼ cup olive oil
1 clove garlic, minced

 ADD MEAT!   Add slices of ham, prosciutto or turkey to add meat.

 MAKE IT VEGAN!   Replace the cheese with Moxarella from the "Substitutions" section.

 GO PALEO!   Replace the bread and cheese with paleo substitutes from your supermarket.

 GLUTEN-FREE!   Use gluten-free bread.

Lemon Garlic Mushrooms over Rice

ACTIVE TIME: 10 MINUTES • TOTAL TIME: 25 MINUTES • SERVES 4

A personal favorite, this dish allows three wonderful flavors to showcase how well they work together.

1. Cook brown rice according to package instructions and set aside.

2. In a small bowl, mix together the garlic, parsley, olive oil and a pinch of pepper. Toss the mushrooms in and set aside.

3. Preheat your grill to medium-high heat and place the mushrooms on the grill. Grill for about 5 minutes and flip. Grill the other side for about 5 more minutes or until tender.

4. Remove the mushrooms, let them cool and dice them. In a large serving bowl, toss the mushrooms, ginger mixture and rice. Serve and enjoy.

1 cup brown rice
1 pound large fresh mushrooms
3 cloves garlic, minced
3 tablespoons parsley, minced
2 tablespoons olive oil
Pepper, to taste

 ADD MEAT! Double the garlic mixture and brush 1 pound of skinless, boneless chicken on both sides. Grill until thoroughly cooked through, about 5–6 minutes per side.

 GO PALEO! Replace the brown rice with Cauliflower Rice from "Substitutions."

 GLUTEN-FREE! Replace the brown rice with quinoa or white rice.

Grilled Goat Cheese Sandwich

ACTIVE TIME: 15 MINUTES • TOTAL TIME: 30 MINUTES • SERVES 4

Goat cheese really has a hold on my heart. I love the tanginess and how wonderfully it mixes with sun-dried tomato pesto.

8 slices whole wheat bread

½ cup sun-dried tomato pesto

1½ cups roasted red peppers, drained and dried

8 slices mozzarella cheese

½ cup goat cheese, crumbled

1 cup baby spinach

¼ cup butter, softened

1. Spread butter on one side of each piece of bread. Evenly distribute the pesto between four slices of bread, spread the pesto on the unbuttered side. If you don't have time to make tomato pesto, slices of a large tomato will be just as delicious!

2. Layer the peppers, mozzarella, goat cheese, and baby spinach on top of the pesto. Place the remaining bread on the top, buttered side up.

3. Preheat your grill to medium heat and place the sandwiches on the hot grates. Cook for 3–4 minutes per side, or until the bread has become golden brown and the cheese has melted. Remove from heat and serve.

 ADD MEAT! Add slices of prosciutto or ham to this sandwich.

 MAKE IT VEGAN! Replace the cheeses with Moxarella from the "Substitutions" section, and replace butter with 3 tablespoon of olive oil.

 GO PALEO! Use paleo bread. Additionally, replace the cheese with any paleo cheese from "Substitutions."

 GLUTEN-FREE! Use gluten-free bread.

Artichoke Panini

ACTIVE TIME: 10 MINUTES • TOTAL TIME: 25 MINUTES • SERVES 2

Grilled artichokes and grilled bread make this a charred delight. Be sure to press the panini with a spatula to get those beautiful grill marks.

1. Spread butter on one side of each of the four slices. On the unbuttered side add a slice of cheese, artichokes, salad greens and a slice of tomato. Place the top piece of bread on top, buttered side out.

2. Preheat your grill to medium heat and place panini on the grates. Grill until bread begins to brown. Flip and repeat. Press down with a spatula to flatten the sandwich. Remove from heat once cheese has melted and the bread has toasted to your liking, and serve.

4 slices multigrain or whole wheat bread

4 slices pepper jack cheese

½ cup artichoke hearts, rinsed, drained and halved

½ cup mixed salad greens

2 slices tomato

1 tablespoon butter, softened

 ADD MEAT! Add a few slices of ham to each panini before grilling.

 MAKE IT VEGAN! Replace pepper jack cheese with Moxarella from "Substitutions." Replace butter with 2¼ teaspoons olive oil.

 GO PALEO! Find an almond-based, paleo-friendly bread at your local super-market and use it instead of Italian bread. Remove the cheese from the recipe.

 GLUTEN-FREE! Use gluten-free bread instead of Italian bread! This kind of bread can be found at most supermarkets.

Cilantro Pesto Sandwich

ACTIVE TIME: 20 MINUTES • TOTAL TIME: 40 MINUTES • SERVES 4

I love the way the cilantro shines in this pesto, setting it apart from the traditional fare.

⅔ cup packed fresh cilantro sprigs

¼ cup packed fresh parsley sprigs

2 tablespoons grated Parmesan cheese

2 garlic cloves, minced

2 tablespoons water

1 tablespoon pine nuts

1 tablespoon olive oil

2 large bell peppers, sliced

4 slices eggplant, sliced ½-inch thick

½ teaspoon salt

¼ teaspoon pepper

½ cup shredded mozzarella cheese

4 rolls

1. Make your pesto by placing cilantro, parsley, Parmesan cheese and garlic in a food processor. Pulse these ingredients until they are sufficiently chopped and slowly add water, oil and pine nuts until the mixture is blended evenly.

2. Preheat the grill to medium heat and brush oil onto the bell pepper slices and eggplant slices. Place peppers and eggplant on the grill. Turning occasionally, grill peppers for 10–15 minutes and eggplant for 3–5 minutes. Once the peppers are tender, remove from heat and set aside. When the eggplant is tender, sprinkle mozzarella cheese over the top and grill for another 2–3 minutes, or until the cheese has melted.

3. Remove eggplant from grill and begin assembling sandwiches. Spread the pesto evenly on the rolls. Top with eggplant and peppers. Serve immediately.

 ADD MEAT! Cook 1 pound of skinless, boneless chicken breast. Grill over medium heat for 5–6 minutes per side, or until tender. Slice the grilled chicken up and add it to the sandwich.

 MAKE IT VEGAN! Replace the cheese with a vegan-friendly substitute from the "Substitutions" chapter.

 GO PALEO! Replace cheese with paleo-friendly cheese from a supermarket. Additionally, serve these with paleo bread or on a Paleo Tortilla, also found in the "Substitutions" chapter.

 GLUTEN-FREE! Serve this on gluten-free bread.

Grilled Corn over Pasta

ACTIVE TIME: 20 MINUTES • TOTAL TIME: 30 MINUTES • SERVES 8

Grilled corn is super easy and always sweet and tasty. The extra smoky flavor that comes along with grilling makes this pasta dish even better. It can be served over pasta, quinoa, rice, or anything you like!

4 large ears corn, shucked

1½ cups uncooked penne pasta

2 cups cherry tomatoes, halved

1 medium zucchini, sliced into ¼-inch thickness

⅓ cup white wine vinegar

2 tablespoon olive oil

1 tablespoon fresh basil, torn

1 teaspoon sugar

1 teaspoon salt

¼ teaspoon garlic powder

¼ teaspoon pepper

1. Cook pasta according to package instructions. Drain and set aside.

2. Preheat grill to medium heat. Brush olive oil on corn and zucchini slices and place them directly on the grill. Turn the vegetables and grill for about 8 minutes, or until they become lightly charred. Let them cool for a bit and then cut the kernels from the cob into a large bowl, adding the zucchini slices, pasta and tomatoes as well.

3. In a small bowl, make the dressing by combining the remaining ingredients. Drizzle over the pasta and toss to coat. Serve hot or cold.

 ADD MEAT!   This is great with flank steak! Prepare the steak for grilling by brushing with olive oil and sprinkling with salt and pepper. Grill each side for about 6 minutes (rare) over medium heat, or until desired tenderness. Dice and add to the pasta.

 GO PALEO!   Replace pasta with "Cauliflower Rice" from the "Substitutions" section.

 GLUTEN-FREE!   Replace pasta with quinoa or white rice!

Eggplant Parm

ACTIVE TIME: 15 MINUTES • TOTAL TIME: 20 MINUTES • SERVES 4

This is a grilled take on the classic eggplant parm. It's quick and simple and will leave you wanting eggplant on the grill everyday! Make this as an appetizer or as a full meal.

1. Preheat grill to medium-high heat. Oil the grill to prevent sticking. Cut each eggplant lengthwise into four pieces.

2. In a small bowl, mix together the olive oil, butter, garlic and parsley. Add a pinch of salt to the mixture, to taste. Use this mixture to coat the eggplant slices.

3. Place eggplant on the hot grates and grill until the slices are tender. This should take about 8 minutes. Sprinkle one side of the zucchini with Parmesan cheese. Remove from heat and serve.

3 medium eggplant
1 tablespoon olive oil
2 tablespoon butter, softened
2 cloves garlic, minced
1 tablespoon parsley, chopped
½ cup Parmesan cheese, grated
Salt, to taste

 ADD MEAT! Add chicken or use it to replace the zucchini. Coat 1 pound of skinless, boneless chicken in the same way you'd coat the zucchini and grill for 5-6 minutes per side, or until it is completely cooked through. Top with Parmesan cheese and cook until cheese melts.

 MAKE IT VEGAN! Use Moxarella or Vegan Parmesan Cheese from "Substitutions." Replace the butter with 1½ tablespoons of olive oil.

 GO PALEO! Use the paleo cheese options found at your local supermarket.

Mushroom Fajitas

ACTIVE TIME: 15 MINUTES • TOTAL TIME: 30 MINUTES • SERVES 4

These tasty fajitas are a great everyday meal, and mushrooms are an obvious addition to this classic dish.

4 large portobello mushrooms
1 large bell pepper, sliced
½ large yellow onion, sliced
3 tablespoons olive oil
1 tablespoon white wine vinegar
1 tablespoon fresh parsley, chopped
2 teaspoons lemon juice
1 clove garlic, minced
½ teaspoon dried basil
¼ teaspoon crushed red pepper
2 tablespoon lime juice
4 flour tortillas
½ cup cheddar cheese, shredded

1. Make the salad dressing in a small bowl by mixing together olive oil, vinegar, parsley, lemon juice, garlic, basil and crushed red pepper. Set aside.

2. Prepare the mushrooms by removing the stems and scooping out the gills. Cut the mushrooms into ½-inch slices and add them to a large bowl. Mix in the pepper and onion and toss to coat with the salad dressing. Let the mixture stand for about 10 minutes to allow the dressing to soak into the mushrooms.

3. Preheat your grill to medium-high heat and lightly oil a grill basket. Place the vegetables in the basket and grill covered for 10–12 minutes, stirring occasionally.

4. Remove from heat when the vegetables are tender and add them to the large bowl. Drizzle them with lime juice and serve on tortillas. Top with cheddar cheese and any other toppings you like.

 ADD MEAT! Add 1 pound of lean ground beef, cook and stirring the beef in a skillet with olive oil until it turns golden brown. Add to your fajitas.

 MAKE IT VEGAN! Remove the cheddar cheese and replace it with one of the vegan options found in the "Substitutions" section.

 GO PALEO! Use Paleo Tortillas (from the "Substitutions" section) and replace the cheddar cheese with a paleo substitute from your supermarket.

 GLUTEN-FREE! Use Paleo Tortillas.

Grilled Eggplant Pizza

Pizza on the grill is something really special. The smoky flavors that enter the dough just make it that much better.

1 pound pizza dough

2 tablespoon olive oil

2 small eggplants

3 small tomatoes

½ cup basil leaves

½ cup mozzarella cheese

Salt and pepper, to taste

1. Begin by separating your pizza dough in half and creating two 10-inch rounds. If the dough shrinks, just wait about 5 minutes before attempting to stretch it again.

2. Preheat your grill to medium heat and brush the top of each round with oil.

3. Slice eggplant into ¼-inch strips and cut the tomatoes into wedges. Brush both the eggplant and tomatoes with olive oil. Season with salt and pepper. Grill the eggplant slices covered until they become tender. This will take about 6–8 minutes— be sure to flip halfway through. Additionally, grill the tomatoes for about 4 minutes, also flipping halfway through. Check for slight grill markings and tenderness. Keep these covered on a plate while cooking the dough.

4. Cook the dough oiled side down, covered. Once the bottoms become crisp and the tops begin to bubble, brush the tops with olive oil. It should take about 2 minutes for the dough to become crisp. Flip the dough over and grill for another 2 minutes.

5. Once the dough is nice and crispy, remove from heat and top with the grilled eggplant and tomatoes, sprinkling mozzarella and basil over the top. Slice and serve.

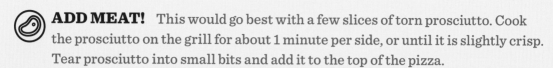 **ADD MEAT!** This would go best with a few slices of torn prosciutto. Cook the prosciutto on the grill for about 1 minute per side, or until it is slightly crisp. Tear prosciutto into small bits and add it to the top of the pizza.

 **MAKE IT VEGAN!** Use the Moxarella recipe from "Substitutions."

 **GO PALEO!** Use the Paleo Pizza Dough recipe from "Substitutions."

 **GLUTEN-FREE!** Use any gluten-free pizza dough from "Substitutions."

Grilled White Personal Pizza

ACTIVE TIME: 10 MINUTES • TOTAL TIME: 25 MINUTES • SERVES 4

I've said it before: Personal pizzas make sharing much easier. There's no fight over that last delicious slice!

1 pound pizza dough

4 tablespoons olive oil

2 cloves garlic, minced

1 cup mozzarella

2 red bell peppers, cut in strips

½ red onion, sliced

¼ cup goat cheese, crumbled

¼ cup Parmesan cheese

6 basil leaves, torn

1. Preheat grill to high heat and brush the surface with some oil. Separate the dough into 4 equal parts. Spread into roughly 8-inch rounds, let sit for about 5 minutes and stretch again.

2. Place the dough on the grill and cook with lid closed for about 2 minutes, or until it becomes slightly browned. Flip and grill for another 2 minutes. Make sure the dough is golden brown and has slight grill marks. Remove from heat to add toppings.

3. Brush olive oil over the bell pepper strips and grill for about 4 minutes, turning the slices halfway through. Lightly brush olive oil over the cooked dough and sprinkle garlic over top. Evenly distribute the mozzarella, cooked bell peppers, onion and goat cheese over the pizzas.

4. Place the pizzas back on the grill and cook until the cheese has melted. Remove from heat and garnish with Parmesan, basil leaves, salt and pepper. Slice and serve.

 ADD MEAT! Add cooked bacon bits to the top of the pizza.

 MAKE IT VEGAN! Use the Moxarella recipe to replace mozzarella in the recipe. Additionally, make some Vegan Parmesan to replace Parmesan cheese.

 GO PALEO! Use the Paleo Pizza Dough recipe, and remove mozzarella and Parmesan.

 GLUTEN-FREE! Use either gluten-free dough recipe to make this pizza gluten-free!

Grilled Eggplant "Pizzas"

ACTIVE TIME: 15 MINUTES • TOTAL TIME: 1 HOUR 15 MINUTES • SERVES 4

Not to be confused with an actual pizza, this is still a lovely way to enjoy saucy, cheesy, beautiful eggplant.

3 pounds eggplant

3 tablespoon salt

⅓ cup extra virgin olive oil

Pinch of ground pepper

½ cup mozzarella cheese

15 ounces pizza sauce

Parmesan cheese

1. Cut your eggplant into ½-inch slices, sprinkling salt on both sides of every slice. Place the slices in a colander over your sink or a bowl. Let this stand for one hour to drain. Rinse the slices under cold water and place on several layers of paper towels to press the water out.

2. Preheat your grill to medium-high heat. Brush both sides of the slices with olive oil and sprinkle with some ground pepper. Place your slices on the grill and cook one side until it is slightly browned, taking 5–6 minutes.

3. Once that first side has cooked, flip the slice over and remove from heat to add sauce and cheese. Distribute sauce and mozzarella cheese over the grilled side of the slice.

4. Place eggplant back on the grill to cook the other side and melt the cheese. Remove from grill, top with Parmesan cheese and serve.

 ADD MEAT! Grill up a few slices of prosciutto and tear the slices, spreading evenly across the eggplant pizza.

 MAKE IT VEGAN! Use the Moxarella recipe from "Substitutions."

 GO PALEO! Make this paleo by replacing the cheese with Macadamia Ricotta from "Substitutions."

Pineapple Pizza

ACTIVE TIME: 15 MINUTES • TOTAL TIME: 20 MINUTES • SERVES 2

This is a classic summertime favorite and surefire crowd-pleaser.

1. Prepare your grill for medium-high heat. Cut pineapple into ¾-inch-thick slices and grill for about 5 minutes on each side, or until lightly charred. Once properly cooked, remove from heat, cut into small cubes and set aside.

2. Increase the grill temperature to high. Spread out dough to approximately 10 inches around, or to desired thickness. Spread olive oil generously atop dough. Place the dough oil-side down directly onto the grill. Cook on this side for 2-3 minutes with the lid closed, making sure the dough becomes golden and charred.

3. Once adequately grilled, coat the top side with oil and flip the dough over. Quickly spread pizza sauce on top and add pineapple, mozzarella and cilantro (or parsley). Close the lid and cook for about 5 minutes. Be sure to turn the pizza about 2 minutes in to ensure that it is evenly cooked. Once cheese is melted and the dough becomes slightly crispy, remove from heat and serve.

7-ounce room temperature pizza dough

½ cup fresh pineapple slices

5 ounces shredded mozzarella

2 tablespoons cilantro or parsley, chopped

½ cup pizza sauce

3 ounces olive oil

 ADD MEAT!   Add ¼ cup of bacon or ham and add with the cilantro and parsley!

 MAKE IT VEGAN!   Remove cheese from the recipe, it tastes just as good without it! Or use the Moxarella recipe in the "Substitutions" section.

 GO PALEO!   Remove the cheese and make pizza dough using the Paleo Pizza Dough recipe in the "Substitutions" section!

 GLUTEN-FREE!   Make the dough using the Gluten Free Pizza Dough recipe (in "Substitutions").

Tomato and Goat Cheese Pizza

ACTIVE TIME: 15 MINUTES • TOTAL TIME: 25 MINUTES • SERVES 4

The tanginess of the goat cheese adds a delicious component to this classic pizza. Its smooth texture meshes beautifully and the smoky flavors from the grill make this a can't-miss dish.

1. Let the dough thaw and separate into four equal parts. Flatten them into small discs of equal size. They should be about ¼-inch thick.

2. Preheat your grill to medium heat. Brush the discs with olive oil on both sides and place on grill. Cook only one side for 2–3 minutes. Once cooked, remove from heat and let cool.

3. Brush the tomatoes with oil. Grill tomatoes for about 1–2 minutes. Do not flip them while grilling.

4. In a small bowl, combine goat cheese, basil, salt and pepper and spread on the grilled side of your pizza crust. Top with the grilled tomatoes and put the pizzas back on the grill for 4 more minutes. Remove from heat and serve.

32 ounces frozen dough
5 large tomatoes, thinly sliced
1 cup goat cheese
½ cup basil leaves, chopped
Pinch of salt and pepper
½ cup olive oil

 ADD MEAT! Sprinkle cooked, torn slices of ham over the pizzas when you top them with the additional toppings.

 MAKE IT VEGAN! Simply remove the cheese or replace the cheese with Moxarella from "Substitutions."

 GO PALEO! Remove the cheese from the pizza and replace the dough with the "Paleo Pizza Dough" recipe from "Substitutions." You can also replace the cheese with Macadamia Ricotta Cheese.

 GLUTEN-FREE! Replace the pizza dough with either gluten-free dough recipe in "Substitutions."

Artichoke Pizza

ACTIVE TIME: 20 MINUTES • TOTAL TIME: 25 MINUTES • SERVES 4

Not to be confused with the pizza chain, this recipe gives you the tools to enjoy your own artichoke pizza without leaving your house.

1 pound pizza dough

2 tablespoons olive oil

1 cup artichoke hearts

3 cups baby spinach

½ cup basil leaves

½ cup mozzarella cheese

Salt and pepper, to taste

1. Begin by separating your pizza dough in half and creating two 10-inch rounds. If the dough shrinks, simply wait about 5 minutes before attempting to stretch it again. Brush the top of each round with oil.

2. Slice artichokes in half and preheat your grill to medium heat. Brush both the artichokes with olive oil and season with salt and pepper. Grill the artichokes, covered, until they become tender—making sure to flip halfway. This will take about 6–8 minutes. Check for slight grill markings and tenderness. Keep these covered on a plate while cooking the dough.

3. Cook the dough oiled side down, covered. Once the bottoms become crisp and the tops begin to bubble, brush the tops with olive oil. It should take about 2 minutes for the dough to become crisp. Flip the dough over and grill for another 2 minutes.

4. Once the dough is nice and crisp, remove from heat and top with the grilled artichokes and baby spinach, sprinkling mozzarella and basil on top. Cook for 2 more minutes, slice and serve.

 ADD MEAT! Sprinkle cooked bacon bits over the pizzas for an additional topping.

 MAKE IT VEGAN! Simply remove the cheese or replace it with Moxarella from "Substitutions."

 GO PALEO! Remove or replace the cheese and use the Paleo Pizza Dough recipe from "Substitutions."

 GLUTEN-FREE! Replace the pizza dough with either gluten-free recipe in "Substitutions."

Thai Veggie Pizza

ACTIVE TIME: 20 MINUTES • TOTAL TIME: 40 MINUTES • SERVES 4

One rarely finds Thai pizza anywhere, but when done right it offers a delightful alternative to the more traditional flavors we all love.

1 pound pizza dough

1 medium eggplant

2 small zucchini

2 bell peppers (any color)

¼ small red onion

6 white corn tortillas

1 medium avocado, sliced

¼ cup cilantro, minced

¼ cup olive oil

¼ cup cheddar cheese, shredded

Thai Peanut Sauce from the "Marinades & Sauces" section

1. Begin by slicing eggplant, zucchini, bell peppers and onion into approximately ¾-inch-thick strips. Try to keep them approximately the same size so cooking times will stay similar.

2. Preheat your grill to medium-high heat. Brush the sliced vegetables with olive oil, place them on your grill and cook until tender. Cooking times may vary; eggplant and zucchini should take about 4–5 minutes per side, bell peppers about 2 minutes per side and onion about 3 minutes per side. Check for tenderness and slight grill marks. Remove from heat and slice into bite-sized cubes.

3. Raise grill to high heat and brush the surface with some oil. Separate the dough into 2 equal parts. Spread each part into roughly 10-inch rounds, let sit for about 5 minutes and then stretch again to desired size.

4. Place the dough on the grill and cook with lid closed for about 2 minutes, or until it becomes slightly browned. Flip the dough and grill for another 2 minutes. Make sure the dough is golden brown and has slight grill marks.

5. Make the peanut sauce by following the steps in the "Marinades & Sauces" section, under "Thai Peanut Sauce." Toss all of the grilled vegetables in 3 tablespoons of the sauce in a large bowl.

6. Distribute vegetables evenly between the two pieces of dough, sprinkle cheese on top and place on the grill for about 2 more minutes. Slice and serve.

ADD MEAT!   Sprinkle cooked bacon bits over the pizzas for an extra savory topping.

 MAKE IT VEGAN!   Simply remove the cheese or replace the cheese with Moxarella from "Substitutions."

 GO PALEO!   Remove the cheese from the pizza and replace the dough with the "Paleo Pizza Dough" recipe from "Substitutions."

 GLUTEN-FREE!   Replace the pizza dough with either gluten-free recipe in "Substitutions."

Three Cheese Pizza

All this cheese makes this a bit of a guilty pleasure, but it's really easy to add veggies and protein as well.

1 pound pizza dough

1 cup mozzarella cheese

½ cup pepper jack cheese

2 tablespoons goat cheese, crumbled

1 teaspoon dried basil

1 teaspoon oregano

Salt and pepper, to taste

1. Begin by separating your pizza dough in half and creating two 10-inch rounds. If the dough shrinks, just wait about 5 minutes before attempting to stretch it again.

2. Brush the top of each round with oil. Cook the dough oiled side down, covered. Once the bottoms become crisp and the tops begin to bubble, brush the tops with olive oil. It should take about 2 minutes for the dough to become crisp.

3. Flip the dough over and pile on the cheese. Make a base of mozzarella and sprinkle pepper jack and goat over the top. Cook for about 3 minutes, or until cheese begins to melt. Sprinkle with basil and oregano, serve and enjoy.

 ADD MEAT! Sprinkle cooked bacon bits over the pizzas when you top them with the additional toppings.

 MAKE IT VEGAN! Replace the cheese with Moxarella from "Substitutions."

 GO PALEO! Remove the cheeses from the pizza and replace them with paleo cheese. Replace the dough with the Paleo Pizza Dough recipe from "Substitutions."

 GLUTEN-FREE! Replace the pizza dough with either gluten-free recipe in "Substitutions."

Grilled Portobello "Pizzas"

ACTIVE TIME: 10 MINUTES • TOTAL TIME: 25 MINUTES • SERVES 4

These are some mini personal pizzas without the dough. Top them with any pepper you like, but I prefer to use banana peppers for an extra kick. These portobello pizzas are an easy and fun way to eat mushrooms with your hands!

1. In a large resealable bag, mix together oil, garlic and vinegar. Once you've combined the mixture, place the mushroom caps in the bag and let them marinate for 1 hour.

2. After the caps have marinated, fill them with about ¼ cup of tomato sauce and top with freshly grated mozzarella. Top them with banana peppers and Parmesan.

3. Preheat grill to medium heat and place the caps on the grill for about 10 minutes, or until cheese melts. Remove from heat, top with torn basil leaves and serve.

8 large portobello mushroom caps, stems removed

¼ cup olive oil

4 cloves garlic, minced

2 tablespoons balsamic vinegar

2 cups tomato sauce

8 ounces mozzarella cheese, grated

4 ounces Parmesan Cheese, grated

½ cup spicy banana peppers, sliced or chopped

Fresh basil leaves

 ADD MEAT!   Top the mushrooms with ⅓ cup of pepperoni slices to enhance the savory flavor.

 MAKE IT VEGAN!   Replace the cheese with Moxarella from "Substitutions!"

 GO PALEO!   Remove the cheese and replace with a paleo cheese from the supermarket. Additionally, if the sauce you are using isn't paleo, use the Paleo Pizza Sauce recipe in "Substitutions."

Lemon Vegetables over Rice

ACTIVE TIME: 30 MINUTES • TOTAL TIME: 1 HOUR 30 MINUTES • SERVES 4

The lemon marinade, mixed with the smokiness from the grill, infuses the rice with so much additional flavor. I love to make enough for a whole week's worth of dinner.

1 cup uncooked brown rice

¼ cup lemon juice

¼ cup soy sauce

2 tablespoon sesame oil

3 cloves garlic, minced

1 tablespoon chives, minced

1½ teaspoon ground ginger

1 pound cremini mushrooms

2 bell peppers

1 medium summer squash

1 small red onion

1 pint cherry tomatoes

1. Cook brown rice according to package directions. Set aside.

2. For your marinade, mix lemon juice, soy sauce, sesame oil, garlic, chives and ginger in a small bowl. Continue mixing until marinade ingredients have blended evenly.

3. Prepare the vegetables by cutting the bell peppers into bite-sized chunks and the onion into wedges. Place the vegetables in a large, resealable bag, add the marinade and toss to coat. Let the bag stand in the refrigerator for at least 1 hour. After an hour, remove the vegetables and save the remaining marinade. Thread the vegetables onto skewers in any order you prefer.

4. Preheat grill to medium heat and lightly oil the grates. Place the skewers on the grill and cook, covered, for 6–8 minutes, turning occasionally. While the vegetables are grilling, baste the skewers with the remaining marinade to enhance the flavor. Remove from heat when everything is tender and serve over brown rice.

 ADD MEAT! Double the marinade and reserve half in a large bag. Add 1 pound of skinless, boneless chicken to the marinade and sit in the refrigerator for 1 hour. Grill the chicken until tender, about 5 minutes per side.

 GO PALEO! Use Cauliflower Rice instead of brown rice and coconut aminos instead of soy sauce.

 GLUTEN-FREE! Use quinoa or white rice instead of brown rice. Instead of soy sauce, use coconut aminos or tamari to make the sauce gluten-free.

Index

About the Author

Elizabeth Orsini is a Fordham graduate currently living in Boston. Her desire for delicious and healthy food, paired with her love of cooking for others, has taught her to adapt to any palate, diet or preference. She now works as a biomechanical engineer thankfully living with fewer hungry mouths!

About Cider Mill Press Book Publishers

Good ideas ripen with time. From seed to harvest, Cider Mill Press brings
fine reading, information, and entertainment together between
the covers of its creatively crafted books. Our Cider Mill bears fruit twice a year,
publishing a new crop of titles each spring and fall.

VISIT US ON THE WEB AT
www.cidermillpress.com

OR WRITE TO US AT
12 Spring Street
PO Box 454
Kennebunkport, Maine 04046